MAKE A MILLION LOOK SMALL

MAKE A MILLION LOOK SMALL

Shift Your Mindset to Multiply Your Wealth

DR. PEGGY McCOLL

Bestselling author of *THE MOMENT OF ALIGNMENT*

Published 2026 by Gildan Media LLC
aka G&D Media
www.GandDmedia.com

MAKE A MILLION LOOK SMALL. Copyright © 2026 by Dr. Peggy McColl. All rights reserved.

No part of this book may be used, reproduced or transmitted in any manner whatsoever, by any means (electronic, photocopying, recording, or otherwise), without the prior written permission of the author, except in the case of brief quotations embodied in critical articles and reviews. No liability is assumed with respect to the use of the information contained within. Although every precaution has been taken, the author and publisher assume no liability for errors or omissions. Neither is any liability assumed for damages resulting from the use of the information contained herein.

Front cover design by David Rheinhardt of Pyrographx

Interior design by Meghan Day Healey of Story Horse, LLC

Library of Congress Cataloging-in-Publication Data is available upon request

ISBN: 978-1-7225-0736-7

10 9 8 7 6 5 4 3 2 1

To Kayla

This book is dedicated to you, with a heart full of gratitude and love. You are more than a partner in my business; you are family in the truest, deepest sense. As the brilliant wife of my son Michel and the devoted mother of my precious grandchildren, James and Aria, you hold a place in my life that is beyond words.

Your wisdom, your presence, and your love enrich my world every single day.

This book is a celebration of possibility, and you embody that spirit beautifully.

With all my love,
Peggy

Contents

Foreword by Phillip B. Goldfine   11
Acknowledgments   15

Part I

The Principle   17

The Spark of a Million   19
Why a Story?   23
The Power Within   27

Part II

The Story   31

Scene 1   The House That Started It All   33
Scene 2   The Morning after the Dream   37
Scene 3   The First Threshold   41

Scene 4   Clay to Mold   45

Scene 5   The Battle between Belief and Desire   49

Scene 6   The Bold Ask   53

Scene 7   The Terror and the Knowing   57

Scene 8   The Battle You Can't See (but Must Win)   61

Scene 9   The Party before the Proof   65

Scene 10   When the Sky Opens   69

Scene 11   When the Dream Arrives Dressed in Reality   73

Interlude   From Story to Self   77

Part III

The Practice   79

1 Decide As If It's Done   81

2 Live the Image Until It Feels like Memory   85

3 From Doubt to Dominion   91

4 Move in Alignment   95

5 Let the Dream Lead You   99

6 Hold the Frequency   103

7 The Effortless Thought   107

8 Stories That Make a Million Look Small   111

9 Do What You Love and the Money Will Follow   119

Contents

10 The Secret Key of Worthiness 123
11 Your Relationship with Money 127
12 Fear as Fuel 131
13 The Questions That Make a Million Look Small 135
14 Reduce It to the Ridiculous 139
15 The Most Precious Commodity 143
16 The Power of Persistence 147
17 The Stream Must Flow 151
18 The Gestation Period 155
19 The Calm of Completion 159
20 The Currency of Imagination 163
21 Play in Possibility 167
22 Anchor the Identity 171
23 Wealth Anchors 175
24 Act As If, Live As Now 179
25 Celebrate before Arrival 183
26 The Million Made Small 185

Note from the Author 189
About the Author 191

Foreword

by Phillip B. Goldfine

IF THERE'S ONE THING I have learned from decades in Hollywood—producing everything from Oscar-winning documentaries to thrillers and comedies—it's this: success belongs to those who decide it's theirs. Not someday. Not when circumstances seem convenient. But now. Success is born in the moment a person chooses to claim it, holds a vision larger than the world around them, and commits to living from that vision with unwavering conviction.

It's my pleasure to write this foreword for Peggy's book, because she is someone who truly embodies what I just described. When inspiration calls, she answers. And she doesn't hesitate—she moves with clarity, energy, and decisiveness. That ability to act on inspiration is one of the many reasons Peggy has achieved such extraordinary success throughout her life.

Peggy and I officially met many years ago when she launched a seminar entitled Making a Million Look Small. I can still remember sitting in the front row, captivated by her words and presence. It was one of those rare moments where you know you are witnessing something powerful in the making.

Fast forward to today, and here we are again—with Peggy once more demonstrating the same spirit of bold, decisive creation through this remarkable book.

Since first meeting Peggy, I've had the joy of sharing stages with her, developing programs together, and being mentored alongside her by the legendary Bob Proctor. Bob's questions and insights weren't lifelines for us—they were sparks, igniting fires that were already burning. Peggy and I are both living proof that anyone can make a million look small when they choose to step fully into the power of their own mind.

I recall one particular moment at a Bob Proctor seminar when he suddenly invited me to step up and deliver an Oscar acceptance speech—even though I hadn't yet won. It wasn't play-acting; it was embodiment. It was a rehearsal for inevitability, a way of stepping into the reality I was destined to experience. That moment was not frightening—it was affirming. It became living evidence that imagination precedes creation, the principle that runs through every page of this book.

Peggy has built her life and her legacy on this truth: who you choose to *be* comes before what you get to *have*. She doesn't simply talk about these principles; she demonstrates them. I've spent countless hours with her discussing how to expand prosperity, elevate consciousness, and open new streams of income, and I've always been struck by her consistency. Time and again, she shows up as the living example of her own message.

This book is not just words on a page. It is a trusted companion, filled with wisdom, guidance, stories, and real-life demonstrations that will stretch your thinking and expand your sense of what's possible. My encouragement to you is simple: don't just read these pages—live them. Practice them. Breathe them in until they become second nature. Because when you do, you'll find that the principles here can transform not only your financial life, but every area of your existence.

A million dollars? It's not the ceiling. It's only the stepping stone. And as Peggy so brilliantly demonstrates, the real journey isn't about the money—it's about the magnificence you discover in yourself along the way.

Here's to your expansion, your prosperity, and to making a million look small.

Phillip B. Goldfine is an Academy Award, Tony Award, and Emmy Award–winning producer.

Acknowledgments

WHAT TRULY MAKES MY life fulfilled—what some might call "rich," but rich indeed, rich in love, rich in joy—is my family.

My husband, Denis, my soul mate, the man I am so blessed to share this life with.

My son, Michel, whom I love unconditionally and wholeheartedly.

My two extraordinary grandchildren, James and Aria, who bring boundless joy and wonder to my world.

And Kayla, my cherished daughter-in-law, to whom this book is lovingly dedicated. When they come to visit, and the house is filled with their presence, I often find myself texting Kayla after they leave just to say, "My heart is full." That is exactly what they do: they fill my heart with so much love and joy.

I also want to acknowledge my dear friend, Phil Goldfine, who graciously wrote the foreword for this book. He is not only a cherished friend but someone I deeply love and appreciate.

There are many more family members and friends I could mention by name, and my heart overflows with gratitude for them all. In the spirit of keeping these pages focused, I will simply say:

Acknowledgments

I am blessed with an abundance of friendship, support, and love, and I never take it for granted.

To my publisher, G&D Media, thank you for believing in this book and for sharing it with the world. To my wonderful agent, Dan Strutzel, I am grateful for your faith in me and your representation.

And finally, to my readers, my clients, and all those I have the privilege of serving—you are my inspiration. You are the reason I write, teach, and dedicate my life to this work.

To the great master teachers whose words and wisdom continue to guide us—Bob Proctor, Neville Goddard, and many others—thank you for paving the way, for your unwavering dedication, and for reminding us all the power that lies within.

I live a truly blessed life, and I know it. For that, my gratitude is eternal.

Part I
The Principle

The Spark of a Million

THE IDEA FOR *Make a Million Look Small* was not born in a boardroom, or during some polished seminar, or while sketching out numbers on a spreadsheet. It was born in a conversation—a simple, unforgettable exchange with my friend and mentor Bob Proctor.

At the time, I was standing on the edge of a decision that both thrilled and terrified me. I had fallen in love with a home—a beautiful, spacious property that lit me up every time I thought about it. The only challenge? It cost a million more than the home I was currently in. Although I was no stranger to manifesting great things, I could feel the weight of that number pressing down on me, whispering all the reasons why it was "too much."

When I shared this with Bob, he didn't blink. He didn't lean forward in his chair or offer a long explanation. He simply looked at me with the piercing clarity he was known for and said, "A million is neither big nor small. Thinking only makes it so. If you want the house, Peggy, get the house. You're the only one standing in your way."

That was it. A few words. But they landed in me like a lightning strike. He hadn't told me anything I didn't already know deep in my bones: he simply reminded me of a truth I had temporarily forgotten: numbers are neutral. Desire is divine. And the only limits are the ones we choose to accept.

I walked away from that conversation with a fire in my spirit. I began to see a million not as a mountain, but as a stepping stone. I stopped treating it as "a lot" and started treating it as *normal*.

At the time, my existing home had been sitting on the market for thirteen months with no offers and very few visitors. By all appearances, the chances of it selling seemed remote. But after Bob's words lit that fire in me, I decided to act as though the new home was already mine. I called my real estate agent, told him to schedule a showing for the property I desired and insisted that he bring the paperwork with him. He reminded me that we hadn't yet sold our current home, but I was adamant. I asked him to trust me and to bring the paperwork anyway.

We visited the home, and we signed an offer that very day—conditional on selling our house within two weeks. My agent thought I was out of my mind, but he went along. The first week passed with no movement. Then he suggested an open house. Only three nosy neighbors showed up, clearly not buyers. But the very next day, an out-of-town buyer requested a showing. We said yes, even though we were about to leave for a trip to San Francisco and the Napa Valley with friends.

On the eleventh day of the fourteen-day clause, we boarded our flight. By the time we landed, I had multiple voicemails and text messages from my agent: we had received a firm offer, nearly full price. We accepted, which meant the new home was officially ours.

Here's the important part: when I put in that offer, I did not yet have the funds. What I did have was *alignment*. I saw myself living in that new home, easily paying for it, and I stayed anchored in that vision. As always, when you remain unwavering, the Universe rises to meet you. The funds came, through my work, in ways that could only be described as miraculous.

That experience taught me something I have never forgotten: when you move in alignment with your desire, even when the evidence hasn't yet appeared, life rearranges itself in ways that defy logic but feel completely natural once they arrive.

The experience with the house was living proof of what Bob had reminded me—and it set the stage for everything that came next. That shift in perspective changed everything. In the months that followed, I launched a project that generated over $5 million in new revenue. And it wasn't even from my main business. It was an additional stream of income that flowed with such ease that it astonished even me.

Here's the part I need you to hear: I did not grow up with this way of thinking. I wasn't born into wealth or privilege. I was raised in a family where my parents worked relentlessly just to make ends meet. My father, in the latter part of his career, was a janitor. My mother worked as a grocery store cashier. They were good, hardworking, responsible people. They did everything they could to provide for us. But money was always tight. Struggle was familiar. It would have been so easy—so natural—to assume that was the only way life could be.

Yet something inside me refused to settle for that. Somewhere along the way, I realized: *it doesn't have to be this way.* Wealth, opportunity, and abundance were not reserved for "other people." They were available to anyone willing to believe, to desire, and to act in harmony with that desire.

That is why this book exists. To remind you of what is already true: you have infinite potential within you. You are not limited by your background, your bank account, or your present circumstances. You have the same power to manifest $1 million—or $10 million—as you do to manifest $10. The laws of creation do not distinguish between "big" or "small." Only our thinking does that.

Here is what I want you to remember as you turn these pages: desire is the starting point. Not wishing, not vague hoping, not half-hearted interest. Desire. Real, soul-stirring, burning desire. The kind Napoleon Hill wrote about in *Think and Grow Rich*. Desire is not wrong. It is not greedy. It is the natural language of your spirit, whispering to you what is already possible.

This book is an invitation to honor that desire. To see it as sacred. And to learn how to live in such alignment with it that the results become inevitable.

If I can do it—coming from a home where struggle was the norm, where we had no evidence of wealth, where my parents worked their fingers to the bone just to pay bills—you can do it. If I could take Bob's reminder and allow it to expand into millions of dollars, you can too.

The question is not, *can you?* The question is only, *Will you allow yourself to believe it is possible? Will you give yourself permission to want it, to expect it, to receive it?*

Because the truth is this: the million you desire is not "big." It is not "far." It is waiting. And this book will show you how to make it look small.

Why a Story?

WHEN I CONCEIVED THIS book, I knew it couldn't be only a manual or only a memoir. It needed both: a living story you can feel and a field guide you can use. So you'll first step into a narrative that expresses the principles viscerally and then move into more than twenty chapters of practice—clear tools, frameworks, and repeatable moves that translate the story into your daily life.

Why? Because human beings are wired for story. We remember stories long after we forget facts. We feel them in our bodies. We carry them in our hearts. They slip past our defenses and show us truths that no lecture could ever make stick.

Think about the great teachers of history. Ancient storytellers used parables to pass on wisdom. Aesop revealed truths through fables. Napoleon Hill wove his principles of success into the stories of men who embodied them. And Bob Proctor? He gave me formulas, yes, but more than that, he gave me stories that made those formulas come alive. One sentence in particular changed everything: "A million is neither big nor small. Thinking only makes it so." In that moment, it wasn't the words alone: it was the story they carried about possibility, permission, and freedom that struck me profoundly.

I know something about you, the reader: you are not here simply for information. If you were, you could type "how to make a million" into a search bar and scroll for hours. You are here because you want transformation. And transformation comes when the truth is no longer just in your head, but in your bones.

That is why I have written this book in three parts. First, I will set the stage—the spark, the truth, the possibility. Then you will step into a story. Not *my* story this time, but a fictionalized journey that mirrors what every dreamer, every believer, every manifester has faced: the dance between desire and doubt, faith and fear, imagination and reality. You will walk with a woman who dares to believe in something bigger than her current circumstances. You will feel her terror, her leaps of faith, her moments of divine guidance. You will live with her as the impossible becomes inevitable. As you do, something remarkable will happen: you will begin to see yourself in her. Her story will become *your* story. Her triumph will whisper to your soul that it is possible for you too.

This approach may feel risky. It is not the way most books on wealth and manifestation are written. But I have learned to trust my intuition, and my intuition told me this was the way.

Intuition is our soul speaking through us. It is the quiet voice beneath the noise, guiding us when logic cannot. It is the compass that never fails, if we dare to listen. Again and again in my own life, I have proven that when I follow that inner guidance, I am led to miracles I could never have planned on my own.

I invite you to read this book with your heart open. Let the story move you. Let it bypass the intellect and stir something deeper. Know that the truths it carries are eternal, and they are for you.

Here is what I believe with all my being: *if you can think it, you can have it.* Every idea you hold in your mind is evidence of what is already possible for you. You would not be able to conceive of it if it were not available to you in some dimension, waiting for you to claim it.

Is it true, then, that if you think about having $1 million—or $10 million—you can have it? Absolutely, positively yes. This book will not only show you why that is true, it will guide you in experiencing this as truth for yourself.

As Napoleon Hill wrote in *Think and Grow Rich*, "Remember, no more effort is required to aim high in life, to demand abundance and prosperity, than is required to accept misery and poverty."

The Power Within

I ONCE HEARD A statement that has lived inside me ever since: "Everything you need is within you now."

When I first heard those words, I nodded politely. They sounded inspiring, but at the time they felt abstract, almost poetic. Was it possible that everything is already within me? I believed I still needed more experience, more education, more opportunities, more resources. I thought I had to wait until something or someone outside of me appeared before I could move forward.

Over the years—and through many bold leaps of faith—I discovered how literally true that statement is. Everything you need *is* already inside you. The answers. The clarity. The wisdom. The courage. The creative ideas. The inspiration to take the next step. The power to manifest. The vision of what you desire, and the energy that will call it to you. All of it lives in you, here and now, before the circumstances, before the evidence, before the money, before the manifestation.

The challenge is not that you don't have it. The challenge is that we often sit back, hoping someone else will swoop in with the solution. We imagine the perfect mentor, the right book, the podcast, the program that will finally "fix it" for us. Although those teachers and resources can be powerful, they only work when we are ready to receive them. The real breakthrough comes the moment we stop waiting to be rescued and instead recognize that the guidance we seek is already stirring within us—often simply waiting to be sparked or mirrored by something outside of us.

That is what intuition really is. It is the inner compass that never leaves us, the quiet voice beneath the noise, always present, always pointing us back toward our highest path. Mentors, books, podcasts, and programs may remind us of what we already know, but intuition is the source. It whispers. It nudges. It offers a sense of knowing that cannot be explained, only trusted.

Intuition is rarely loud or forceful: it does not shout or demand. Instead, it whispers. It nudges. It tugs gently at our awareness, offering a sense of knowing that cannot be explained but can always be trusted.

I have learned to follow this voice. Sometimes it speaks through stillness, when I am quiet and relaxed, when my mind is not racing to solve a problem. Sometimes it comes in the middle of a walk, when I am not even thinking about the thing I most want an answer to, and suddenly there it is: a clear direction, a flash of insight, a deep certainty. And sometimes it comes through the words of another, reminding me of what I already know to be true.

That is how it was with Bob Proctor. He did not give me anything I didn't already have. He reminded me of a truth my soul already carried: a million is not big, and it is not small. Thinking only makes it so.

Isn't that the essence of all manifestation? What we hold in our mind, with belief and with feeling, becomes what we hold in our hands. If you can imagine it, you can have it. Not because of magic, not because of chance, but because the same Infinite Intelligence that placed the desire in your heart also planted within you the power to fulfill it. The two are inseparable.

This is why I am so passionate about desire. Some people are ashamed of wanting more, as if it makes them greedy or ungrateful. But desire is not a sin. Desire is sacred. Desire is the language of the soul calling you higher. It is the signal of what is possible for you, a preview of the life already waiting in the unseen. Napoleon Hill called it a "burning desire," and he was right. Without it, nothing ignites. With it, everything is possible.

Here's the truth: the moment you allow yourself to want something with your whole being, the way is already made. You may not see the steps. You may not have the resources. You may not understand *how*. But the *how* is not your job. Your job is to live in the vision, to feed the faith, to listen to the whispers of your intuition, and to trust that the Universe will deliver.

I have seen this happen over and over—in my own life, and in the lives of countless others I have taught, studied, mentored, and worked with. I have watched people go from scarcity to abundance, from doubt to confidence, from fear to faith—not because their circumstances changed first, but because they changed within. They began to live as though it were already done. They began to believe that the power was in them. They began to act as though a million was small.

When they did, miracles followed.

This is what I want you to understand before we move into the story at the heart of this book: you are already equipped. You already have the power. You are not missing anything. The dream that stirs in your heart is there because it is yours to claim.

As you turn the page and step into the journey of a woman who dares to follow her desire, remember that her story is not just her story. It is yours too. Her fears will look familiar, because you have faced them. Her doubts will sound like echoes of your own. And her triumphs will awaken something in you—the realization that you are capable of just as much, if not more.

Because everything you need is within you now.

Part II
The Story

Scene 1

The House That Started It All

IT WAS THE KIND of house that didn't just sit by the water: it *belonged* to it. Glass walls drinking in the view, a deck stretching out like open arms, the kind of shoreline that makes you forget your own name for a moment. She had seen it first in a glossy magazine spread, a "City's Dream Home" feature she'd flipped through absentmindedly in a waiting room.

The page stopped her cold. Her breath caught in that way it does when something speaks directly to you before your mind has time to catch up.

The caption said it was a private residence on the market for a "discerning buyer," priced well into the millions. She could barely bring herself to look at the number—a price tag that belonged in another galaxy from where her bank account lived.

Two weeks later, as if fate had been eavesdropping, she drove past an *"Open House"* sign at the edge of a quiet road she rarely took. She followed it without thinking, tires crunching on the gravel drive. And there it was: the house from the magazine, only now it was breathing in front of her. The lake shimmered behind it like an accomplice.

She stepped inside and felt her chest expand and ache all at once. Every detail felt as if it had been whispered into existence just for her: the sunlit reading nook overlooking the dock, the massive floor-to-ceiling stone fireplace that seemed to hum with warmth, the kitchen where you could cook barefoot on the heated floors and watch the sunset melt into the water.

By the time she reached the upstairs master suite, she knew. She didn't just *want* this house. She wanted the life it represented: a life where she could choose beauty without flinching at the bill, where her days flowed with ease, creativity, and freedom.

Yet reality was blunt. Her savings were . . . modest. Her income covered the life she had, not the one this house invited her into. It was, by every reasonable calculation, out of reach.

That night, curled on her sofa with a mug of tea gone lukewarm, she remembered a line from a book called *The Demand Principle*—her own shorthand for this moment. To *demand*, by definition, is "an insistent, peremptory request made as if by right." In other words: ask from alignment, not from lack.

"Demand the answer. Go to sleep relaxed in the knowing that the way is already there. Expect it. It will be given."

It had sounded poetic once, almost too simple to be serious. But now, with the ache of that house still lodged in her rib cage, it read like an instruction. So she decided. No pleading. No bargaining. No "please."

Tonight, she would demand it—not rudely, but with the authority of someone claiming what was hers in another realm already. She would sleep with the knowing, the quiet conviction that the path to that house—or something even better—was already written.

She didn't know what would happen. But she knew this: she was done letting the dream sit in a magazine or behind a "sold to someone else" sign.

She turned off the lamp, lay back against her pillows, and whispered into the dark, *"I demand to feel the certainty that this home is already mine."*

Scene 2

The Morning after the Dream

She woke before sunrise, the edges of sleep still clinging to her like a soft veil. For a few seconds she hovered in that delicious in-between space where dreams and reality blend, not entirely certain where one ended and the other began. The air in the room was cool; the first light of dawn was painting faint gold lines across the wall. She could feel her heart still beating a little faster than usual, as if it were trying to keep pace with the energy of whatever had just happened.

Then she remembered. It came back in a rush—not just the images but the feeling. The night before, she had followed an impulse so strong it had felt more like a command. She had settled into bed, released the day's noise, closed her eyes, and demanded certainty. Not a half-hearted request. Not a timid "please." But a clear, unshakable declaration: "I demand to feel the certainty that this home is already mine." She had gone to sleep anchored in that knowing—a quiet conviction that the way already existed and would reveal itself in perfect time. And it had.

In her dream, there was a presence—she couldn't name it exactly, but it felt both familiar and immense. It didn't tell her what to do in a list of numbered steps. Instead, it painted an entire scene for her to experience. She was in that waterfront home—*her* waterfront home—and every detail was alive. The scent of fresh coffee from the kitchen. The warmth of sunlight spilling across the hardwood floors. The sound of water lapping gently against the dock. Her laughter, unforced and free, filling the rooms. The knowing in the dream was so absolute, so undeniable, that there was no space for doubt.

It was as if the being in her dream had said, *Stop rehearsing the problem. Stop narrating the reasons it can't be yours. Live in the result now—in every thought, every word, every decision. When you do, the path will be shown.*

She sat there in bed, staring at the ceiling, letting the message settle in. It reminded her of a passage she had underlined years ago in *The Moment of Alignment*:

> You must feel the destination into existence. When your inner world is calibrated to the result, the outer world will catch up in ways that appear effortless.

She had understood it back then—at least intellectually. But now she *knew* it in her bones.

Swinging her legs over the side of the bed, she reached for her journal. The pages were cool under her fingertips. She didn't write about the things she didn't yet have or the numbers in her bank account. She didn't let her pen drift into the familiar "someday" language she'd used in the past. Instead, she wrote in the present tense, as if she were already living inside the dream.

She described the view from the bedroom window, the way the morning light danced on the lake, the sound of footsteps on the dock as she carried her coffee outside. She wrote about the peace, the abundance, the security—and how natural it all felt.

The more she wrote, the more her energy began to shift. It was subtle at first, like the slow lifting of fog, and then it became unmistakable. Her shoulders dropped. Her breathing deepened. She could *feel* the alignment happening, the way a compass needle swings toward true north.

This wasn't just a dream to remember. It was an assignment. A starting point. A new operating system. She closed the journal, ran her hand across the cover, and whispered to herself, "It's already mine. Now I simply get to meet it."

With that, she rose to begin her day—not as a woman chasing a dream, but as a woman already living it.

Scene 3

The First Threshold

By midmorning, the glow of her dream was still with her—but so was the world. Her phone lit up with a notification from her banking app: a reminder of an upcoming payment she hadn't planned for. The number on the screen felt like a bucket of cold water thrown over her freshly warmed resolve. The old voice—the one she thought she'd left behind—showed up without knocking. *See? You can't even cover this without juggling things. And you think you're going to buy a million-dollar waterfront home?*

She almost laughed. Almost. Instead, she placed the phone face down on the counter and closed her eyes, taking the same deep, steadying breath she had taken the night before when she'd made her declaration.

The dream's presence was still there, not as vividly as when she'd been sleeping, but as a quiet hum just beneath her thoughts. She heard it—or maybe felt it—reminding her: *Do not measure the vision against your current resources. Measure it against your current identity.*

Identity. That word had been circling in her mind since dawn. It was exactly what she'd heard in her dream:

The size of your result will never exceed the size of the self you are willing to become.

She put the kettle on for chai, one of her grounding rituals. The rhythm of water boiling and leaves steeping gave her a pause to choose her state with intention rather than slipping into the old conditioning of lack.

With the mug warm in her hands, she opened her journal again. She flipped to the page where she'd described the lake house and read it slowly, letting the words repaint the image in her mind.

She noticed something she hadn't the first time: she had described the version of herself in that house as calm, decisive, and generous. Not once had she mentioned her bank balance or her "readiness."

If that version of her existed—and she believed it did—then today's small financial speed bump was simply an irrelevant detail on a much bigger map.

She decided, right there, to treat the rest of the day as a field test for her new identity. What would the "lake house her" do with this morning's bill? She wouldn't panic. She wouldn't spiral. She'd either find the solution or create it, with the same energy she'd bring to choosing a new piece of art for the living room.

The answer came in minutes, almost too quickly for her to believe it. She remembered an overdue invoice from a client she hadn't followed up with—one polite email later, they replied with an apology and a promise to send the payment that afternoon.

Was it magic? No. It was alignment. She had shifted her state first, and then the solution appeared. Not the other way around.

By evening, she was back on the dock in her mind, watching the sun set over water she didn't yet own—but now it felt less like longing and more like inevitability.

Before bed, she whispered the same words she had the night before: *Strengthen my knowing until it feels natural.* And she knew she would dream again.

Scene 4

Clay to Mold

THE NEXT MORNING DIDN'T feel magical. It felt ordinary in the kind of way that can make a person doubt they'd ever touched something extraordinary. Sunlight streamed through her bedroom window, the same way it had yesterday and the day before. She had to remind herself—this is where the real test begins. Not in the high of the vision, but in the low hum of real life.

She reached for her journal, the one she'd scribbled in at 2:37 a.m., when she woke from the dream so vivid it still pulsed in her chest. The memory of it wasn't fading the way dreams usually do—it was holding, anchored, as though it belonged to her.

Then there were the words. Not heard with her ears exactly, but delivered in the deep, confident timbre of a man's voice. It was loud without volume, inside her without echo. She hadn't so much listened to it as absorbed it—as if the meaning bypassed sound altogether and dropped straight into her bones.

Your circumstances are clay, not stone. What you hold in your mind shapes them, but only if you hold it long enough for the shape to set.

She read the sentence in her journal three times, feeling it settle into her.

Her phone was already buzzing with the demands of the day—emails, notifications, a text from a colleague asking if she could "just help out" with a project that had nothing to do with her.

The old version of her would have said yes automatically. This version paused, heard the echo of that inner voice, and asked herself, *Does this move me toward the waterfront home, or away from it?*

The answer was obvious. She typed a polite no, hit *send*, and felt a rush of energy she hadn't expected. It wasn't about the task she'd refused; it was about signaling to herself that she was willing to guard the gate.

The words from the night before continued to unspool in her mind as she drove to meet a friend for lunch. Another line had arrived in that strange, soundless way: *one clear outcome, one aligned action.* She whispered it aloud before stepping out of the car, letting it settle into her posture.

Lunch was lovely, but the real turning point came when her friend mentioned a small networking gathering that night—real estate investors, creative entrepreneurs, and people "with money to play with."

Normally, she would have brushed it off with a quick, "Oh, that's not really my scene." But this time, she felt the nudge. Her clear outcome was ownership of that waterfront home. An aligned action might be meeting someone who could open a door she didn't even know existed. She went.

It wasn't glamorous. The lighting was harsh, the appetizers forgettable, and half the conversations were surface-level. But then she found herself beside a woman who had built a thriving design business from scratch—and had done it while raising two kids and moving countries twice. They talked for an hour.

Somewhere between the second and third story, the woman leaned in and said, "When you get really clear on your vision, the path unfolds in ways you can't predict. But you have to act on the invitations when they come. Most people don't." Her heart skipped. It was almost word for word what that mysterious voice had said to her in the dream.

On the drive home, she realized something important: the dream wasn't the magic. The magic was in taking the instructions seriously when the day looked ordinary, when the path felt murky, and when the opportunities didn't arrive gift-wrapped.

That night, before bed, she wrote in her journal:

"I followed the nudge. I said no to what doesn't align. I said yes to what might. This is how the clay starts to change shape."

Then, just as she had on that first night, she lay down, relaxed her whole body, and said to herself with certainty: "Show me the next right step."

Scene 5

The Battle between Belief and Desire

She hadn't meant to drive by the house again. But something about that morning—the clarity of the light, the soft tug in her chest, the way the breeze moved as if it had a secret—made her turn left instead of right. She told herself it was just a detour. A quick glance. Five minutes, ten tops. Just to see it. But that was a lie.

Her desire for that house had grown from a flicker into a full blaze. She had stood inside it once already, just weeks earlier, during an open house she wasn't financially "qualified" to attend—at least not according to her bank account. But she had gone anyway.

The minute she stepped across the threshold, it was as if the house recognized her. Every detail—the soaring ceilings, the view from the dock, the way the sun filtered through the great room windows as if it knew how to land—felt personal. Intimate. As if the house had been waiting for her and only her.

She pulled slowly into the driveway this time, almost sheepishly, as though she were returning home after being away. For a moment she just sat there, hands resting on the wheel, letting her imagination drape itself over the scene. She pictured stepping out of the car with groceries, humming as she carried them inside. She saw herself setting down her keys on the kitchen counter, the scent of chai steeping in the background. She imagined the creak of the garage door as she wheeled her bike out for a ride along the tree-lined trail, and later, tying her kayak to the dock after a long paddle across the lake. Each image settled into her chest not as fantasy, but as rehearsal for the life that was already reaching for her.

She let herself feel it—not as a someday dream, but as a *now* reality. She leaned back in the seat and closed her eyes. And for a few seconds, she *was* that woman. The one who lived there. The one who bought it without panic, who furnished it with love, who invited people over not to impress but to *share*. The one who had made a million—and then made it look small.

But when she opened her eyes again, the dream cracked. Because she still didn't know how. No road map. No strategy. No obvious deal, investor, or sale waiting in the wings. Her accounts told one story. Her heart told another. And the two were locked in a tug-of-war that was starting to fray her spirit.

She heard the familiar, toxic whisper rise: *who do you think you are?* Her throat tightened. She gripped the steering wheel until her knuckles blanched, nails biting into the leather. Tears welled, heavy and hot, pressing hard against the dam of her determination. Only a couple escaped, sliding down her cheek like proof of the battle raging inside.

She reached for her phone, opened the notes app, and began typing without editing:

I don't know how. I truly don't. But I know that desire doesn't lie. And this one—this house, this life—it's mine. I don't need to force it. But I also won't ignore it. There's a way. There's always a way. My job is not to figure it out. My job is to align.

The words steadied her a little. She sat back. Breathed. Watched a couple walk past with their golden retriever, waving politely as if she *did* live there. That wave meant more than they knew.

She drove home slowly, the kind of slow that listens, that pays attention. She wasn't just driving home. She was rehearsing the route. Memorizing the journey. Anchoring the desire so deeply it could no longer be shaken by logic.

That night, she stood in front of her bathroom mirror and said aloud, "I don't know how—but it's done. Show me the next move."

Then she turned off the light, crawled into bed, and whispered her final thought into the dark: *I'm listening.*

Scene 6

The Bold Ask

She didn't sleep much that night, but it wasn't restlessness. It was reverence. There was a current running through her body—a quiet, golden charge that made her skin feel alive, like a violin string tuned to a frequency she had only just discovered. The memory of that dream, that voice, still echoed in her cells. Not a sound exactly, but a presence. A masculine certainty that didn't shout, didn't rush, didn't beg to be believed. It just *was*. *Go back*, it had said. *Go back and claim it.*

She rose at dawn, pulled on jeans and a soft sweater, braided her hair the way she used to when she needed clarity, and got in the car. She didn't check her bank account. She didn't rehearse logical reasons why this was a waste of time. She just drove. One step. One whisper of trust. One bold act of alignment.

The morning mist was lifting when she turned down the road that led to the lakefront. The trees arched overhead like an honor guard, and as she rounded the final bend, there it was again—*the house*—sitting like a secret only the brave were allowed to remember.

She pulled over slowly and turned off the ignition. The silence pressed in, soft and clean. She let her eyes trace the lines of the roof, the symmetry of the windows, the gentle slope down to the water's edge. Once again she imagined herself stepping out of the garage, helmet in hand, wheeling her bike out for a Sunday ride. She pictured herself on the back deck, coffee warm in her palm, wrapped in a shawl as the sky turned pink and gold above the rippling lake.

She let herself *feel* it: it wasn't a fantasy, but she felt it as a memory pulled forward in time. Then, just as quickly, the old tug returned. The voices. The math. The how-in-the-world-is-this-even-remotely-possible refrain that had lived in her since girlhood. It didn't come shouting. It came with its clipboard and calculator. It came with its audit of facts and its measured disdain for miracles.

Be responsible, it said. *Be reasonable.*

She gripped the steering wheel tighter. Her knuckles began to turn white, but her heart didn't shrink. "This is not a battle between reality and fantasy," she said aloud. "This is a choice between fear and faith."

She sat there a long time. Long enough for a jogger to pass, long enough for a few birds to land and leave the fence posts. Then she did something bold. Not reckless. Bold.

She had already reached out to a real estate agent a few weeks earlier, just to test the waters. The agent had been kind, professional, and eager to help, sending her a handful of listings that were ... fine. Respectable homes. But they were all firmly in the range the agent assumed she could afford, and not one of them stirred her soul. None of them were *this* house.

Now, sitting in her car at the edge of the driveway, she opened her phone and drafted a message. Her heart raced, but her fingers moved with certainty.

I'm putting in an offer. This home is mine. See listing #11999334.

No numbers. No conditions. Just the declaration. When she pressed send, her hands trembled—not entirely from fear, but from release. In that moment, she stopped asking how and started showing up *as if*.

As she drove away, she didn't play music. She didn't need to fill the space. A new frequency was humming around her now, and she knew enough not to drown it out.

The *how* hadn't shown up yet. But *she* had. And that, she realized, is always the first step of a miracle.

Scene 7

The Terror and the Knowing

THE MOMENT SHE SIGNED the offer, her entire body lit up in contradiction. Her hand had moved with conviction, almost serene in its stillness. But the second the pen left the page and the agent smiled with congratulations, something in her stomach dropped like a stone into dark water.

What have I done? Heat rushed up her neck, a metallic taste in her mouth—the body's old alarm—while the signature she couldn't take back dried on paper.

She didn't say it out loud. She didn't say anything. She smiled faintly, nodded, made polite noises, and slipped out the door as if she were moving underwater.

The house, her house—if the offer was accepted—shimmered in the distance like a mirage. Still impossibly beautiful. Still the dream. But now it had teeth. Now it demanded a response that was more than desire. It asked for belief at a level she had never accessed before.

The drive home was silent. No radio. No phone calls. She couldn't tell anyone. Not yet. Not because she was hiding, but because she knew—instinctively—that the first whiff of doubt from someone else would unravel her. "You did *what?*" they'd say. "Are you out of your mind?" They would mean well—some of them. They would want to protect her. But protection wasn't what she needed. Faith was, and faith is delicate in its early moments. It must be held like a new flame.

Her body felt a wave of pressure and tightened; it wasn't from fear exactly, but from the enormous weight of what she'd just done. It wasn't just a house. It was a line in the sand. An irrevocable declaration to the Universe: *I am not who I was. I am choosing from the place I'm becoming.* Yet the terror was real. God, was it real.

That night, she couldn't eat. She lay on the couch in her favorite blanket, staring at the ceiling, heart thudding so loudly she wondered if the neighbors could hear it. The question looped on repeat in her mind like a cruel lullaby: *what if you can't pull this off?*

She had no rational answer. The bank account did not yet reflect the size of the commitment. The pathways were invisible. No clear plan in motion. No inheritance. No secret fund. And yet . . . and yet . . . she had been here before in spirit. She had practiced this frequency, this flavor of boldness, this surrender. But never with stakes so high. Never with a desire so viscerally alive.

Finally, she did the only thing that had ever given her peace when the world inside her felt louder than the one outside: she went to bed and asked.

This time she didn't whisper. She demanded out loud, with intensity. *Show me. I trust. I've leapt. Now catch me.*

She lay in the dark, palms open on the sheets, breath slow. She wasn't afraid: at this point she refused to bow to fear. She was choosing to allow the unfoldment to occur. It was all still so new—this woman she was becoming—but she knew the terms now. The Universe responded to boldness. To clarity. To movement. To alignment.

Then, just as she began to drift into the space between waking and sleep, it happened again.

The voice.

Not heard with her ears. Not quite a sound. But a presence. A message. A knowing that arrived in the middle of her mind like thunder through silk.

You are not crazy. You are aligned.

It was a man's voice again, clear and calm and utterly confident, echoing through her like scripture carved into bone. She felt it more than heard it. As it filled her, the panic began to subside. The feeling didn't disappear, not entirely. But she became quiet. The way a raging sea settles after a storm—still churning, but manageable. Trustable.

You were led to that house for a reason. It is yours because it called you. You didn't chase it. You remembered it. You remembered who you truly are.

A sob escaped her chest—not from grief, but from relief. From resonance. From the unmistakable sense that she wasn't alone in this. That something far more intelligent than her worry was at work. A force that understood timing and money and miracles far better than her nervous system did.

You don't need to know how it will happen. You only need to know what you want—and you do. Trust in that clarity.

She cried, quietly. This time, the emotion felt calmer. She felt a deep sense of gratitude that invited in a higher feeling of faith.

She drifted into sleep with the words still echoing through her: *The money is already there. Your only job is to know it.*

In the dream that followed, she saw herself walking through the front door of the house, not as a visitor, a hopeful observer, or a potential buyer, but as its owner. She was barefoot. The sun poured through the windows. Music played faintly in the background. She could smell something warm in the oven. She was laughing, not at anything, just because it was real. It was hers. She had remembered this place into being. And it had answered her back.

Scene 8

The Battle You Can't See (but Must Win)

THE OFFER WAS ACCEPTED. Four words. That's all it took to tilt the axis of her entire world. Not in the way she'd imagined—with champagne and a squeal and a moment of dancing in the kitchen—but with a thud. A quiet, irreversible thud that echoed through her rib cage and settled like stone in her gut.

She stared at the email. Read it twice. Then again. And instead of elation, she felt the edges of panic starting to sharpen.

She had done the brave thing. She had said yes to the house—to the life. Now that yes was real. Legally binding, in fact. Her signature was on paper. A deposit was wired. There were dates and terms and lawyers and a seller who had accepted her proposal.

This was not a photo on a vision board anymore. This was real estate. She'd already given notice on her rental to align with the move-in date. If the deal died now, she wasn't just losing a deposit, she was losing her address.

Suddenly, she couldn't breathe. The voices came screaming in—not the kind you hear, but the kind you feel rumbling under your skin. *What have you done? You don't have the money. Not all of it. Not even close. You're going to lose your deposit. You'll get sued. You'll be humiliated. You gave notice on your apartment. If this falls through, you'll be living out of a storage locker and trying to pretend it was all part of your plan.*

She didn't tell anyone. She couldn't. Because she knew what they would say. They would confirm the fear. They would echo the logic of doubt. They would tell her she had lost her ever-loving mind. And the truth was, she wasn't entirely sure she hadn't.

That night, she climbed into bed like someone slipping into a boxing ring—tired before the bell. She closed her eyes and whispered what had become her nightly demand: *deepen my calm and strengthen my certainty.*

And the dream came. It didn't include clouds or wings or scrolls. But with that same knowing voice—loud and steady, and yet somehow not audible at all. A masculine presence, strong and warm, filling the space between her thoughts.

You are not in a financial battle, it said. *You are in a spiritual one. The war is between faith and fear. And only one wins.*

She was silent in the dream, but listening as if her life depended on it. Because it did.

Faith, the voice said, *must be fed.*

Then an image unfolded. She saw herself standing in the kitchen of the lake house, barefoot on the hardwood, sunlight pouring in like a promise. She was making tea. Humming. There were framed photos on the counter. A stack of mail with her name on it in the new address. She walked through the house and out to the dock. The water was still, like breath before a word. She sat. She belonged. There was no striving. Only being. She woke up with tears on her face.

The battle hadn't disappeared. The uncertainty hadn't evaporated. But something inside her had shifted. The voice was right. If faith was to win, it needed nourishment. Starving it by obsessing over timelines and bank statements would be like planting seeds and then yelling at the dirt.

So she got up. She didn't check her balance. She didn't Google mortgage crisis scenarios. She walked to her desk, opened her journal, and wrote: *I am grateful knowing I own my home on the lake. I live in it now. I wake up to the sound of the waves. I sit by the fireplace at night. I feel peace in every room. I belong here.*

She read it aloud. It was vocalized like a declaration. As if she was reading a truth already etched into stone.

Then, every day after, she did it again. She spoke the life into being. She walked around her rented apartment as if it were the lake house. She imagined opening the garage to take her bike down the trails. She envisioned sunset dinners on the deck. She lived there in her mind so vividly that her nervous system began to follow. Her body stopped flinching. Her breath came back. This became an hourly declaration; an obsession.

The fear still visited. It always does. But now she knew what to do with it. She didn't argue. She didn't explain. She just fed faith instead. In those quiet moments, a new conviction began to rise. Not *I hope it works.* Not *I really want it.*

But *it's mine. It's done. I'm living there now.*

Scene 9

The Party before the Proof

SHE HAD NEVER PLANNED a party before buying a house. Not once. Not even for her tiny apartment in the city with its squeaky floors and windows that howled in the wind. Yet, here she was, curled up on the corner of her couch with a stack of custom invitations fanned out on her lap, running her fingers over the raised gold lettering like Braille for the soul.

> HOUSEWARMING CELEBRATION
> *Saturday at sunset*
> *The address of her dream.*
> *The full address. Printed. Inked. Real.*

She hadn't told a soul. Not her sister. Not her best friend. Not even her own reflection, not out loud. Because how could she explain it? She was throwing a party for a home she did not technically yet own. A home she did not yet have the funds to close on. A home that existed, in the eyes of the world, only as an offer awaiting paperwork and fate.

But in her bones, it was hers. She had learned—through trembling nights and soul-deep dreams—that the only path forward was to live from that knowing. Not around it. Not beside it. *From* it.

She sent the invitations. She didn't send an email or a text. Instead she put the invitations in the post, as if it were the 1950s and certainty was made of card stock and postage stamps. She placed each one in the mailbox like a promise to the Universe.

Then she began to plan. She visualized it all in astonishing detail. The warm amber glow of lanterns hanging from the back patio beams. The way her heels would click on the stone path as she answered the door. The hum of jazz in the background, the scent of lemon rosemary chicken wafting in from the open kitchen, and the glint of the lake beyond the French doors catching the evening light as if it were winking just for her.

But most vivid of all were the faces. Her friends and family, stepping over the threshold for the very first time, eyes wide, mouths ajar, voices bubbling with disbelief and delight.

"Wait . . . this is *yours*?"

"You're kidding me."

"How did you do this?"

"When did you . . . ?"

"Why didn't you *tell* us?"

She would smile and pass the guest a glass of chilled champagne. She wasn't smug. Just sure. A quiet, grounded joy rising from her belly.

As she poured imaginary drinks and clinked glasses in her mind's eye, she didn't just see their faces: she felt them. Heard them. The cadence of their laughter. The slight catch in their breath when they stepped into the grand hallway and saw the view of the lake from the living room. Their admiration wasn't the goal; it was the evidence of her alignment. A reflection of her faith. A reward for living inside the miracle before it unfolded.

Each night that week, she walked herself through the party again before sleep. She walked the floors in her mind, lit the candles, fluffed the pillows, and looked out at the water as if she had always belonged there. Then she'd drift into dreams, where the voice returned.

You are the only proof you need, it said one night, low and certain.

Another night: *Those who wait for evidence stay waiting. You create evidence by your willingness to live from the unseen.*

On the morning when she picked up the catering samples, her stomach fluttered. She was feeling a new level of excitement. It was a joyful energy. The frequency of full belief. She reminded herself: this wasn't pretend. This was prophecy.

She was becoming the woman who owned that home—in deed and in identity. And this party, this "ridiculous" leap of faith, as some might call it, was her declaration. Her way of standing fully in the promise before the world handed her the proof.

She didn't need to explain it. She didn't need to justify it. She just needed to keep living it, imagining it so real that it was vivid to her senses.

Within a few days of mailing the invitations a friend texted a photo of the invitation: "Is this for real? Did you already close?" She smiled at the screen, felt the pinch of doubt try to rise, and typed back, "It's real." Then she set the phone down and went back to choosing lanterns.

Scene 10

When the Sky Opens

It was a Tuesday when the email came. The kind of Tuesday where nothing felt exceptional. Her inbox was cluttered with the usual—promo codes, subscription pings, a gentle nudge from the lawyer's office reminding her that the funds for the home must be wired in full no later than two weeks from Friday. She had read that line twice. Then again. Her throat tightened like a pulled drawstring. Friday. Two weeks and four days.

She closed the email and stood still in the kitchen, staring out the window, not seeing the trees beyond it. Her imagination had carried her this far. Her inner work had strengthened muscles that used to tremble at the first sign of fear. But this was something else. This was a wall with no door, no window, no crack of light. The voice within—the one she'd come to trust—was quiet. Not absent, just... waiting.

She placed both palms on the counter and spoke out loud. "I know you hear me. I'm not asking *how*. I'm asking for calm while I trust the unfolding."

Then she walked herself into her vision. Again. She sat in the living room of *her* home—high ceilings, lake breeze through open windows, the warmth of late afternoon sun reaching across her hardwood floors. She could feel the glass of cold lemon water in her hand, the way the condensation kissed her palm. She imagined putting fresh flowers in the ceramic vase on the kitchen island. The view from the dock. Her white robe draped over the back of a chair. She lived there. She *lived* there. In her spirit, it was already hers.

By noon, she was back at her desk. Her hands hovered over the keyboard. She pulled up her email. Something was . . . odd. Emails pouring into her inbox confirming sales.

Dozens of them. Then hundreds. Notifications were flooding her dashboard like a storm surge. At first she thought it was a glitch. Her courses—solid, well-loved—had always brought in a trickle of revenue. But this? This was something else. She opened Instagram, then froze.

There it was. A reel. Bright, punchy, and unmistakably *her*. A prominent influencer—someone with millions of followers—had posted a gushing ninety-second testimonial about how her course had radically changed the way she saw herself, her business, her life. The caption read: "I've done a lot of programs. But this one? This one rewired me. Forever grateful. If she's still selling this, get it. No, seriously. Run."

The comments were on fire. The post had gone viral. And so had the exposure. The sales kept pinging. Then everything stopped. Her payment processor flagged the surge as "unusual activity" and placed a seventy-two-hour hold on disbursements. The number on the screen was more than enough to close, but the funds were frozen behind a progress bar and a polite email from "Risk."

For a full minute her throat closed. Then she pushed the laptop away, put both feet on the floor, and chose: *I'm not moving in fear.* She sat down, grounded herself, closed her eyes, and began to visualize once again. She walked the lake house in her mind. Her breaths were calm: slowing inhaling and exhaling. She was breathing like someone who already lived on the water.

The next few days unfolded like a miracle wrapped in momentum. Her inbox became a symphony—each new sale chiming like a bell of confirmation. She left her laptop open overnight, letting the soft ping of incoming orders lull her to sleep like a lullaby written in the language of abundance.

It was a marvel. She hadn't launched a campaign. No emails had gone out. She hadn't even nudged the influencer—though she would, in time, with a handwritten letter of heartfelt thanks and a meaningful gift chosen with care.

For now, she allowed herself the sacred act of receiving. With open hands, open heart, and open tabs. The Universe had moved, and she had moved with it.

On day two, the influencer's link appeared not to be working, and conversions dipped. She laughed—gently—and, within a matter of minutes, the broken link was fixed. Nothing in her moved.

By the end of the week, the number in her business account exceeded the amount needed for the home. She wired the funds to the lawyer's office, calm and clear.

When she hit *send*, she sat back and let the tears fall. She felt complete reverence. She had walked into the storm of doubt, carrying nothing but her belief and a willingness to follow unseen instructions.

And now the sky had opened. That night she dreamt again. The voice, warm and commanding, filled the space behind her eyes: *Never doubt the force that moves on your behalf when you refuse to move in fear. It is not the world that delivers your desires. It is your alignment that commands it.*

She woke up with the sunrise, smiling.

Scene 11

When the Dream Arrives Dressed in Reality

THE KEY TURNED IN the lock with a click so soft it might have been mistaken for silence, and yet, to her, it echoed through the chambers of her heart like cathedral bells. The door opened—*her* door—and the air inside felt charged, almost sacred. It wasn't the price tag or the glossy, magazine-worthy perfection that made her pause. It was the deeper knowing: this house had already been hers in the unseen, lived in a thousand times within her imagination. And now the walls seemed to whisper back, *we know you.*

She stood in the doorway and did nothing for a long while. No rushing. No calling anyone. No racing to unpack. She just stood there and let the frequency of fulfilled desire wash over her skin.

This wasn't about the granite or the glass or the glint of light bouncing off the water just beyond the wide back windows. It was about the fact that she had *become* the woman who lived here. Not borrowed it, not lucked into it, not talked herself into believing she might deserve it one day. She *was* this woman now.

The movers came and went like polite ghosts. She directed them calmly, with a confidence that surprised even her. Every piece of furniture had already been placed in her mind weeks before.

Every painting, every photo, every color had been curated in the invisible world and now arrived obediently in this one. Her body ached by nightfall, but her spirit was incandescent.

It didn't take long for the house to feel like home. Within just two days, every detail was in order: dishes neatly stacked in the cupboards, towels folded over the racks, beds dressed and waiting, paintings perfectly placed on the walls. By the end of the first week, the transformation was complete, and with it came the moment she had been envisioning all along: her celebration. The very celebration she had dared to plan and invite guests to even before the purchase was finalized.

When the doorbell rang just past six, her breath caught. She'd sent out the housewarming invitations weeks ago with a full heart and a trembling hand, and now the guests she'd seen only in imagination were beginning to materialize in real time.

It was her sister first, standing on the porch with her mouth slightly open and her eyes scanning the trim, the angles, the view. "This is . . . *yours?*" she whispered, stepping into the front hall as if she were entering a temple.

She handed her sister a champagne flute, just as she'd seen in her vision. "Welcome," she said, steady now, smiling like someone who had finally come home to herself.

Within the hour, the living room hummed with voices, laughter, and the sweet undercurrent of disbelief. Friends wandered the hallways in awe, whispering as though the house might be listening. One of them walked out onto the back deck and let out a sound that was half-gasp, half-prayer. "I didn't even know this kind of life was real," she said, holding her phone up to capture the sunset.

A former colleague pulled her aside, eyes wide. "You bought this? When? How? You didn't say anything."

She simply smiled. "I wasn't ready to explain it. I was just . . . aligning with it."

The comment left her friend blinking. But no one could argue with the glow in her eyes or the certainty in her voice.

Throughout the night, she moved through the rooms like someone playing a part they were born to play. Every imagined moment unfolded with uncanny precision—voices where there had been silence, clinking glasses where there had once been longing. The dream had not just come true—it had *become her life.*

Later, alone in her home barefoot and spent but not tired, she looked around at the space that now held her dreams in the walls. She saw the empty champagne flutes in the sink, the scatter of empty plates on the countertops, and sensed the faint trace of perfume lingering in the air. Proof. Evidence of alignment. Of belief that didn't flinch in the face of a bank balance. Of action taken before certainty ever arrived.

She curled up on the window seat and watched the moonlight dance across the water. A soft voice echoed in her chest—booming, steady, now familiar.

You've always lived here. This is not the end. It's the beginning.

As she exhaled, her eyes scanning the silhouette of trees swaying above the lake, she felt the full, sacred truth of what had just unfolded. This wasn't just about a home. It wasn't even about a miracle. This was about alignment so precise, faith so rooted, imagination so real, that what once felt like a mountain now looked like a pebble. She had made the impossible look inevitable. She had made a million look small.

With that, she closed her eyes and slept the deep sleep of a woman who had not only witnessed the miracle—but had *become* it.

Interlude

From Story to Self

YOU'VE JUST READ ABOUT a woman who moved a desire from paper to porch light. You've seen how a house can become a home in the unseen first, how faith can be fed, how identity—once claimed—changes what reality is willing to deliver. None of this was luck. None of it was coincidence. It was alignment.

This next section is where you pick up the thread.

Part II was a mirror: a parable designed to let you *feel* the laws at work without stopping to label them. If aspects of her journey echoed your own—fear tightening when the goal gets real, imagination loosening it again, evidence arriving the moment you stop begging for it—good. That resonance isn't entertainment: it's instruction. It tells you your system already recognizes the path.

Part III is your blueprint. It won't ask you to be perfect. It will ask you to be decisive, consistent, and willing to live as the person who already holds the outcome. The shift is simple to say but profound to live. You are not chasing proof anymore; you are creating it. The *how* reveals itself to the identity you embody, not to the doubt you explain.

Before you turn the page, make three quiet agreements with yourself:

1. **Decision over negotiation.** Decide your dreams are done—every morning, every night. No more bargaining with old stories.
2. **Image over evidence.** Live in the result until it feels like memory. You'll act from it, and your world will reorganize.
3. **Action over anxiety.** Make high-impact moves every day. Small hinges, big doors.

A suggestion for momentum: treat the next seven days as a primer week. Guard your inputs. Feed faith on purpose. Speak your outcome as present, not pending. You'll notice the air change—subtly at first, then unmistakably.

You hold the same power the heroine discovered: everything you need is within you now. Desire is not a defect; it's direction. When you align thought, feeling, and action with that direction, you don't just make progress—you make a million look small.

Turn the page. Let's build.

Part III
The Practice

1

Decide As If It's Done

EVERY GREAT TRANSFORMATION BEGINS with a decision. Not a wish, not a fleeting thought, not a half-hearted "maybe someday," but a decision so solid, so final, that it reshapes who you are in an instant. When you truly decide, something shifts. The old you no longer has the reins. The new you—the one aligned with your desire—takes the lead.

This is the first and most important key to making a million look small. It is the hinge upon which every door of abundance swings open. A genuine decision is the difference between dabbling in desire and embodying destiny. Most people don't actually decide. They hope. They wait for circumstances to give them permission. They tiptoe toward their dreams, testing the waters, afraid to commit in case it doesn't work out. But hoping is not deciding, and waiting is not creating.

A true decision burns the bridges to your old limitations. It is a declaration to yourself and the Universe: *this is who I am now, and nothing less will do.*

But let's be honest: deciding at this level rarely feels calm at first. Burn-the-boats decisions almost always come with a wave of discomfort—sometimes even terror. When I once had my eye on a home that was a full million more than the one I was living in, I didn't leap immediately. I had to "warm up" to the decision. My first reaction wasn't serenity; it was unease. Not because I thought I would fail, but because I genuinely had no idea how to make it happen. It felt like such a big stretch—bigger than anything I had ever stepped into before.

Here's the process I used, and the one I still use whenever the discomfort shows up: I acknowledge it without judgment. I don't pretend it isn't there, but I also don't indulge it. I recognize that fear is simply an emotion, not a prophecy. Then I redirect. I ask myself an empowering question, like, *now that this home is already mine, how does it feel?* That single question shifts me back into alignment with the result. The fear may still whisper, but the faith gets louder.

This is how you move through the discomfort of decision: not by waiting for the fear to vanish, but by choosing again and again to live in the identity of the result you've claimed.

When I say *decide*, I don't mean bargaining with your dream. I don't mean, "I'll try this for a few weeks and see what happens." I mean a burn-the-boats, there's-no-turning-back decision. The kind that says, "I already own this reality within me. I refuse to entertain anything else." You may not know the *how*, you may not know the timing, but when your yes is absolute, the Universe rearranges itself to match your new identity.

Bob Proctor used to say that most people treat their goals like preferences. They treat them as something they'd like to have if it fits neatly into their existing life. But wealth, freedom, a million made small—these things do not come to the hesitant. They come to the decided. When you decide, your whole being starts to organize around that truth. Your thoughts sharpen. Your energy shifts. Your choices align. And suddenly, opportunities that were previously invisible reveal themselves in perfect timing.

Here is the simplest way to test whether you have truly decided: check your language. Do you say, "I want to be wealthy" or "I *am* wealthy"? Do you say, "I hope to attract abundance" or "I live in abundance now"? Do you say, "I want to live in a house like that" or "That is my home, and I own it outright"? The words you use reveal your level of decision. A real decision is not about someday: it is about now.

Every morning and every evening, declare your decision as if it were already done. This is not a ritual of repetition; it is a ritual of identity. Write down a single sentence that captures your decision— your "identity lock." Something like:

> *I am the woman who makes a million look small.*
> *I am the man who attracts abundance with ease.*
> *I am living in the home of my dreams, fully paid for, fully mine.*

Say it with conviction. Feel it resonate in your body. Let it settle into your cells. The morning declaration sets the tone for your day. The evening declaration locks it into your subconscious as you sleep.

This is how you burn the boats daily. You don't give yourself an exit ramp. You don't flirt with old stories of limitation. You reinforce the only truth that matters: *it is done.*

The moment you decide, you become magnetic. You no longer beg reality to change; you command it by your unwavering alignment. You collapse the distance between where you are and where you want to be, because decision makes you one with the result.

That is the starting point of every miracle, every breakthrough, every million made small.

I ask you now, as you hold this book in your hands: *are you dabbling, or are you decided?*

Until you decide that it's done, the Universe can't deliver. Once you do, nothing in heaven or earth can stop what is already yours.

2

Live the Image Until It Feels like Memory

IMAGINATION IS NOT MAKE-BELIEVE. It is creation in its earliest form. What you hold vividly and consistently in the theater of your mind is already as real as anything in the physical world; it simply has not yet hardened into fact. To live the image is to step into your future before it arrives, to wear it like a garment until it becomes as familiar to you as your own skin.

Neville Goddard, one of the greatest teachers on this subject, said it best in his book *The Power of Awareness*. In chapter 24, titled "Failure," he wrote: "The time it takes your assumption to become fact, your desire to be fulfilled, is directly proportionate to the naturalness of your feeling of already being what you want to be—of already having what you desire."

In other words, the more natural it feels to inhabit the reality of your dream, the faster it materializes. If it feels foreign, distant, or like a fantasy, the delay will match that vibration. But when the dream feels normal, inevitable, and lived-in, you collapse time.

Think about it: everything you now take for granted in your life was once only imagined. The home you live in, the relationships you cherish, the work you do each day—all of it existed first as an inner image. You rehearsed it in your mind until it became ordinary to you, and then life caught up. That is the art of manifestation in motion.

Most people make the mistake of holding their dream like a picture on the wall: admired but separate from themselves. They see it as something "over there" in the future, while continuing to identify with the self who does not yet have it.

The work is to reverse that process. You must become the person who has it *now*—in feeling, in imagination, in identity. The dream must become so woven into your inner experience that it feels like memory, not fantasy.

Living the image is not a trick you perform once or twice a day. It is a state you occupy, an atmosphere you carry with you. The point is not to close your eyes for five minutes, conjure up a dream, and then spend the rest of the day contradicting it with fear and doubt. The point is to assume the feeling of the wish fulfilled as your *dominant way of being.*

This doesn't mean you never waver. You are human, and waves of fear or doubt may still visit. But the practice is to return, again and again, to the knowing of already having it until that becomes your baseline. Through consistent repetition, you train your inner state to align with the reality you have chosen. It's the steady act of bringing your whole being into sync with the reality that you've decided is yours.

So if your dream is a home, don't just imagine it in the morning and leave it there. Carry it with you all day. As you drive through traffic, feel yourself as the owner of that home. As you cook dinner, see yourself cooking in *that* kitchen. As you drift to sleep at night, let the last thought in your mind be that you are already living there.

If your dream is financial abundance, then walk through the world as someone who is already financially free. Breathe as that person, speak as that person, choose as that person.

The aim is saturation. You want to dwell in the image so consistently that it is imprinted upon your subconscious as *normal*. Not extraordinary, not far off, but natural. When the dream becomes ordinary in your inner life, it cannot help but become ordinary in your outer life as well.

Consider for a moment how you feel about things you already possess. Do you ever doubt whether your car is yours? Do you ever sit down in your living room wondering if you're truly allowed to be there? Of course not. Ownership is natural. Belonging is unquestioned.

That is exactly how your desires must feel. When you dwell in the naturalness of already having them, they shift from being "out there" goals to "in here" realities. This is the difference between someone who hopes to one day live in their dream home and someone who knows without question that they already do.

This state of knowing magnetizes circumstances, ideas, people, and resources. The world rearranges itself to reflect what you have already claimed inwardly.

This is where so many people misunderstand manifestation. They treat it like a ritual—something to be done for five minutes a day, like brushing their teeth, hoping it will be enough to convince the Universe. But true creation is not born from a few fleeting moments of focus. It is born from a dominant state of being.

This is exactly how I became a *New York Times* bestselling author. Long before it was a fact on paper, I lived in that identity every single day. I imagined myself stepping on stage, hearing the announcer say, "And here is Peggy McColl, *New York Times* bestselling author."

I let myself feel the thrill, the pride, and the normalness of it, until it became so natural inside me that the outside world had no choice but to match it.

I remember watching Rhonda Byrne share how she visualized her book and film *The Secret* sweeping across the world. She didn't "hope" they would be successful. She saw the emails pouring in. She imagined hearing comments from viewers whose lives had been changed. She lived in that image every hour of the day. As you know, the result was history.

This is the kind of commitment world-class performers bring to their vision. Great athletes do it too: they see the victory in their mind long before it happens. They rehearse the result so vividly that when the day comes, it feels inevitable.

It is not about practicing for five minutes—it is about *living* as the person who already has it. The repetition is not in the minutes spent visualizing, but in the constancy of your identity. The assumption becomes who you *are*, not just something you do.

When you make that shift, results no longer come from "trying." They come because reality has no choice but to mirror what has already taken root in you.

One of the simplest and most effective ways to sustain this dominant state is to shape your environment so that it supports your assumption. Your home, your workspace, even the background of your phone or computer can serve as anchors. But let's be clear: these are not "reminders" in the sense of trying to recall something you don't quite believe. They are confirmations—reflections of a truth already established within you.

A framed image of your dream home on the wall isn't a vision board gimmick; it is evidence. A set of car keys you hold before you own the car isn't wishful thinking; it is identity rehearsal. Each cue becomes a mirror reinforcing your conviction until the world has no option but to align.

Manifestation is not occasional: it is continual. It is not about effort: it is about embodiment. When the assumption of already having it feels as normal as breathing, life reorganizes itself in obedience.

The woman who knows she is already the owner of her waterfront home carries herself with quiet authority. The man who knows he already commands wealth speaks with clarity and moves with ease. Their environment bends around their inner state, because identity precedes reality.

As I wrote in *The Moment of Alignment*, "Your ideal life is not somewhere in the future. It's already yours, ready to be realized—right now."

That is the truth we must return to repeatedly. Not forcing, not waiting, not wondering—just being. Living in the now as though it is already complete. In that naturalness, the so-called time delay between desire and fulfillment collapses. The dream ceases to be a dream. It becomes the only possible reality.

3

From Doubt to Dominion

DOUBT IS QUIETER THAN fear, but it is often more dangerous. Fear at least announces itself with pounding heartbeats, sweaty palms, or sleepless nights. Doubt is subtler. It creeps in like a draft under the door, whispering second guesses, planting hesitation, making you question whether what you want is really possible, or, worse, whether you are worthy of it at all.

Years ago, I heard Bob Proctor say something that has never left me: "It only takes a little bit of poison to kill." The poison he was speaking of wasn't physical: it was emotional. Doubt, fear, and worry are poisons of the mind, and if you let them linger, they will choke the life out of a dream. Just as a drop of toxin can taint a clear glass of water, even a little doubt left unattended can cloud your vision and weaken your faith.

This is why I teach the importance of finding the antidote. In my book *Your Destiny Switch*, I showed how human emotions exist on a spectrum, with faith at the high end and fear at the low. When you recognize you've slipped into the lower states of worry, doubt, or fear, the way out is not to resist them but to deliberately shift into their opposite: calm, confidence, and relaxation. That is the antidote. That is how you starve the poison and strengthen the energy that will carry you forward.

Worry is doubt's close cousin. Worry is simply doubt rehearsed over and over again, a kind of negative meditation. It takes your imagination—the very faculty designed to carry you into new realities—and shackles it to the worst-case scenario. Worry is not harmless: it is creative energy turned against yourself. It is like prayer in reverse.

Doubt and worry are thieves of time, energy, and momentum. They don't just cloud the mind, they distort perception.

Opportunities can be right in front of you, but if you are steeped in doubt, you'll overlook them. Solutions can be at your fingertips. but worry convinces you they won't work. When your inner dialogue is filled with *What if I fail? What if it all falls apart? What if I'm not enough?* you are scripting a future you don't want to live.

The antidote is not to fight doubt. Fighting doubt gives it attention, and what you attend to grows. The antidote is to starve it—to feed something stronger in its place: faith, certainty, knowing.

Years ago, I had a client who told me she was overwhelmed by worry every time she took a step toward her dream of starting a business. She would lie awake rehearsing everything that could go wrong: the money running out, her family laughing at her, customers rejecting her. One day I asked her, "If you have the imagination to rehearse the worst, do you also have the imagination to rehearse the best?"

At that moment, her shoulders dropped. She had been using her most powerful tool—her mind—in the wrong direction. The shift didn't come from eliminating doubt. It came from directing her imagination toward a new set of rehearsals: clients saying yes, her bank account filling, her family beaming with pride. Within a year, that business was thriving.

You cannot stop thoughts of doubt from knocking on the door. They will visit. The question is: will you invite them in and serve them tea, or will you let them pass by while you remain anchored in your knowing? Dominion begins when you choose not to entertain the guests of worry and doubt.

Instead of asking, *what if I fail?* ask, *what if this works better than I can imagine?* Instead of whispering, *what if I lose it all?* declare, *what if this is the moment everything changes in my favor?* These questions are not just semantics. They redirect the brain. Neuroscience shows us that the brain is a question-answering machine. Give it destructive questions, and it will generate destructive answers. Give it empowering questions, and it will generate solutions, ideas, and evidence that support your success.

This is the practice of dominion: ruling your inner dialogue instead of being ruled by it. You are not a victim of your thoughts: you are the one who chooses which ones to water. Doubt may arrive, but it does not have to dominate. Worry may visit, but it does not have to unpack its bags.

When you decide to feed faith and starve doubt, you are not pretending challenges don't exist. You are choosing to align with the only frequency that has ever solved anything: faith. Faith sharpens your perception, increases your creativity, and attracts resources that worry would keep hidden.

So the next time doubt whispers, *what if you can't?* answer back with dominion: *what if I already did?* And watch how the energy shifts.

Doubt will always try to shrink your dream, but faith will always expand it. The moment you step into dominion over your inner dialogue, you begin to make even the largest goals—a million, ten million, more—look small.

4

Move in Alignment

WHEN YOU HAVE DECIDED, when you have lived the image, and when you have chosen faith, the next step is movement. Not frantic action, not busy work—alignment.

Alignment comes when your outer steps match your inner knowing. It's when what you think, feel, and do all flow in the same direction, like three streams converging into a single river. This is the power that carries you forward with ease.

Many people make the mistake of separating belief from behavior. They visualize their dream during infrequent fleeting moments and then spend the day contradicting it with actions that don't align. They affirm abundance and then complain about lack. They imagine health and vitality, then treat their body like an afterthought. They declare their decision but live as though they are still waiting for proof. This fracture between inner and outer keeps the dream suspended.

When you move in alignment, everything changes. Every choice becomes a vote for the reality you have already claimed. You begin to behave as the woman who already lives in her dream home, as the man who already commands wealth, as the soul who already walks in freedom. You don't wait for evidence; you act as evidence.

This is not about forcing action or hustling harder. True alignment is not strain: it's flow. It's accepting what feels congruent and avoiding what doesn't. It's listening inwardly and moving accordingly. Alignment often requires less effort than people think, because the right next step always feels lighter than the alternatives. It clicks. It fits.

Think of alignment as tuning a musical instrument. If the strings are too loose or too tight, the sound is off. But when you tune each string to the right pitch, the music flows effortlessly.

Your life is the same. When your thoughts, feelings, and actions are out of tune, the result is dissonance: frustration, delay, stagnation. But when you align them, the symphony plays. Opportunities harmonize. People appear at the right time. The melody of your dream becomes audible in the world.

Alignment often calls for bold moves—the kind that stretch you beyond your comfort zone but are fueled by faith, not recklessness.

I think of the woman in our story who longed for her waterfront dream home. On paper, she wasn't ready. The finances weren't yet in place. Logic told her to wait. But something in her knew this was the home. So she acted in alignment with that knowing. She put in an offer before she had the evidence to support it.

I've done the same in my own life. When I bought my dream homes—and I've bought many—I didn't wait until every detail lined up perfectly. I felt the fear, but I went forward anyway. I called the agent. I signed the papers. I stepped into the reality before the money had appeared, because mentally I was ready. That's alignment: moving boldly in harmony with your inner conviction.

But let's be clear: this is not about blind leaps. Aligned action is not recklessness; it's self-awareness. You must know yourself. You must discern a truly inspired action from a forced attempt to control the outcome. Inspired action carries energy, expansion, and a whisper of inevitability. Forced action carries panic, pressure, and fear. The difference matters.

Not every aligned step looks dramatic. Sometimes the most powerful moves are subtle, exploratory, even playful.

Research is also action. If you were a multimillionaire today, where would you invest? What opportunities would you explore? How would you use your money to grow, give, or create? Begin investigating those things now. Call it a game if you like—the money game. Play it. Look up properties. Browse investment options. Tour neighborhoods. Visit showrooms. Try on the life you've already chosen to live.

These "small" actions are not insignificant. They are demonstrations. They are rehearsals of identity. They signal to your subconscious (and to the Universe itself) that you are preparing, that you are readying yourself, that you are moving in alignment with what you've already claimed inwardly.

One of the easiest ways to test alignment is to notice how you feel when you take action. Does it feel heavy, forced, filled with resistance? Or does it feel clean and expansive, even if it stretches you? The right next step may scare you, but it won't suffocate you. It will carry a sense of truth, like stepping onto a path that was waiting for you all along.

Consider the story of someone who has decided to embody wealth. In alignment, they don't hope to become wealthy someday: they handle money with the precision and confidence of someone who already *is*. They don't shrink from opportunities out of fear; they step toward them, knowing wealth is their natural state. Or think of the woman who has claimed her dream home. She doesn't just imagine it. She begins to move in ways that align with ownership: she curates her environment, she speaks with authority, she even parks her car in the driveway as if it were already hers. That is alignment in motion.

When you move in alignment, you collapse the gap between the unseen and the seen. Life rushes to support the congruent. Misalignment delays, and alignment accelerates.

PRACTICE: THE ALIGNMENT CHECK-IN
Throughout the day, pause and ask yourself three questions:
1. **What am I thinking?** Is it consistent with my decision? Am I thinking as the person who is already living the life I have imagined?
2. **What am I feeling?** Does it match the state of already having my desire(s)?
3. **What am I doing?** Is this action the behavior of the person I've chosen to be?

If the answer is yes, keep going. If not, tune the string. Adjust. Realign.

The Universe always responds to who you are being *now*. When who you are inside matches what you are doing outside, reality has no choice but to reflect your alignment back to you.

Let every step you take become a declaration. Let every word you speak become confirmation. Let your life itself become the proof of what you have already decided is yours.

When you move in alignment, you don't chase results. Results chase you.

dream cannot lead someone who refuses to be led. Faith is required not only to believe in the outcome, but to allow the route to unfold one surprising step at a time.

There is immense freedom in this. No longer do you need to figure out every detail. You no longer need to bully life into submission. You walk in a state of expectancy, knowing the dream is already yours, knowing it is leading you toward itself in ways far better than you could have planned. You trust the process, even when it looks like detour. You trust the timing, even when it feels delayed. In that trust, you discover that the dream doesn't just bring you what you wanted: it brings you what you never knew to ask for.

So let the dream lead. Let it be your compass, your lighthouse, your gentle pull forward. Stay faithful to the image, stay aligned in your being, and walk in readiness. The way may surprise you. In fact, if you are doing this right, it will.

Instead of waiting for evidence, practice responding to life *as if the dream is already accomplished*. When an opportunity arises, ask yourself: *if it's already done, how would I respond?* When you walk into a store, drive your car, or talk with a friend, carry yourself with the quiet confidence of someone who already lives in that reality.

This isn't about setting aside time to practice: it's about living in the assumption, moment by moment. Let your dream lead your posture, your choices, your words, your energy. This is how you allow the surprising way to unfold—not by forcing action, but by embodying the fact that it's already yours.

you confuse the two, you create tension, resistance, and frustration. But when you trust the division of labor—when you let the Universe do what only it can do—everything begins to flow.

Think of it like a dance. Your responsibility is to hold your posture, keep the rhythm, and stay attuned to the music. The Universe leads with the steps. When you try to drag the Universe across the floor, you stumble. When you allow it to guide, you are carried into turns and movements you never could have choreographed yourself.

Bob Proctor often said something that stuck to me like glue: the way your desire arrives will almost always surprise you. Rarely does it march in through the front door, wearing the clothes you imagined. More often, it sneaks in through the back gate, disguised as an unexpected phone call, a chance encounter, a "coincidence" that drops at just the right moment. When you let the dream lead, you stop demanding that it arrive in the exact package you scripted. You allow yourself to be astonished.

This is why surrender is not weakness: it is wisdom. It is the willingness to admit that your dream knows more about its own unfolding than you do. To surrender is not to sit idle; it is to walk in readiness, eyes open, ears tuned, heart soft enough to notice when the dream whispers, *This way.*

Think of your dream as a lighthouse. Its beam may not reveal the whole coastline, but it illuminates the next turn you must take. That one step, when followed in trust, will reveal another, and then another. The dream leads you breadcrumb by breadcrumb. Your only task is to keep moving, even when the path looks nothing like the map you once drew.

The mind, of course, will protest. It will want guarantees. It will argue for control. But if you insist on knowing every turn before you move, you will remain parked where you are, waiting forever. The

5

Let the Dream Lead You

THERE COMES A MOMENT when your dream must change from being something you drag behind you to becoming the thing that pulls you forward. This is the shift from forcing to flowing, from controlling to allowing. You are no longer pushing your way toward the goal, as though it were some mountain you must conquer. Instead, you let the dream lead you, as though it were alive, magnetic, already reaching back to claim you.

This is the paradox of creation: you must decide boldly, act courageously, and align consistently—and then you must release the obsession with the *how*. The *how* is never your job. The how belongs to the field of Infinite Intelligence, the mind that spins galaxies and orchestrates encounters you could never arrange on your own. Your job is to remain faithful to the vision and open to the nudges, impulses, and opportunities that surface in response.

Manifestation is a partnership. You and the Universe each have a role to play. Your role is to live in the end—to embody the reality of your desire as though it is already here. That is your job. The Universe's role is the *how*: the orchestration of timing, people, resources, and opportunities. That is not your job, and it never has been. When

6

Hold the Frequency

ONCE YOU'VE DECIDED, ONCE you've lived the image until it feels like memory, once you've fed the faith and taken aligned action, there comes a crucial part of the process: holding the frequency.

This is the difference between dipping into a state of knowing and *living* there. It is one thing to taste the vibration of your dream fulfilled; it is another to hold it so steadily that it becomes the very atmosphere you breathe. Think of it like tuning a radio dial. You don't flick past the station, hoping to catch a song you like every now and then. You lock it in. You keep it tuned, even when there's static, because you know the signal is there.

Your dream has a frequency—a vibrational signature that matches the feeling of already having it. When you align with that frequency and refuse to waver, you build momentum. Life has no choice but to harmonize with your state.

Contrast will always come. Old paradigms are not eager to let go. They rise up like waves, offering the opportunity for you to either fall back into the familiar or stay rooted in the new. It can feel like a royal battle at times, because those ingrained patterns have been rehearsed for years, even decades. They know how to whisper doubt, how to masquerade as reason, how to press against your faith until you question yourself.

But here's the truth: this very battle is a sign of growth. Resistance often peaks just before the breakthrough. The more you practice living in the naturalness of completion—the more you *feel at home* in the state of "already done"—the weaker that battle becomes. What once felt like a storm becomes a faint breeze. What once knocked you flat becomes barely a wobble. When you practice holding the alignment, the battles lessen, and you experience greater ease with manifesting any desire.

Contrast isn't your enemy; it's the echo of old conditioning. It's proof that you're shifting. Every time you hold steady in the face of it, you rewire your paradigm, you anchor deeper into alignment, and you strengthen your capacity to remain unshaken.

Holding the frequency doesn't mean ignoring contrast. It means standing so firmly in the reality of your fulfilled desire that contrast loses its grip. The more you do this, the more effortless it becomes, until what once felt like struggle dissolves into second nature.

Bob Proctor used to remind me that most people are run by their conditions. They let circumstances control how they feel. Leaders, creators, masters of manifestation flip that dynamic. They let their inner state command the outer world.

Here's where emotional calibration becomes vital. Think of your emotions like a dimmer switch. (I discuss this in more detail in my book *Your Destiny Switch*.) When fear is up, the room of your life grows dim. Possibilities hide in the shadows, even though they're still there. But when faith and certainty are turned up, the light floods in. You see connections, opportunities, resources that were invisible before. Holding the frequency is keeping your inner light on bright, no matter what flickers outside.

Remember the woman from earlier in this book who dreamed of her home by the water. She had no logical evidence that it could happen. Her finances didn't line up, her circumstances seemed unprepared, and every "reasonable" voice around her told her it wasn't the right time. But she tuned her inner dial to ownership. She saw herself walking through those front doors, placing her keys on the counter, and sitting on the back deck as the sun set over the waves.

When she sent a text to the agent to indicate she was ready to put in an offer, her body shook with fear. The facts screamed, *you're not ready*. Yet her faith whispered, *it's already yours*. She chose to hold the frequency of ownership. She put in the offer, trembling but unwavering inside.

What happened? The impossible became possible. Money flowed in from directions she hadn't expected. People appeared with resources, opportunities, and solutions that hadn't been visible before. As Bob always reminded me, the *way* it unfolded surprised her, because the method is rarely what we expect. But the key was this: she never let go of the state. She held the frequency of "already done" until reality had no choice but to catch up.

Holding the frequency is not about straining to stay positive or pretending everything is fine. It's about cultivating such a dominant inner knowing that nothing shakes you for long. You become emotionally resilient. An out-of-alignment feeling may happen—that's natural—but you recover quickly. You reset to alignment again and again until it becomes automatic.

Here are a few ways to anchor that frequency:
- A phrase you return to like a tuning fork: *It is done. It is mine now.* Say it until it feels like the deepest truth.
- A vivid image you can access instantly: walking into your new home, holding the book with your name on the cover, hugging the loved one you've longed to call yours.
- The breath as reset: Inhale certainty. Exhale gratitude. Use it as often as needed.

These aren't five-minute practices you dabble in. This is a way of being. It's the frequency you choose to live in repeatedly, until it becomes as natural as your own heartbeat.

As you hold the frequency, the world bends. Opportunities arrive with uncanny timing. People show up with answers you didn't know you needed. Resources emerge from directions you never considered. The *frequency* draws it in; the method is often beyond your imagination.

This is why holding steady matters so deeply. If you wobble, if you let doubt dominate, you slow down the arrival. But when you stay anchored in the vibration of fulfillment, even when conditions look unchanged, you collapse the delay.

Holding the frequency is not passive. It is active trust. It is fierce relaxation. It is knowing that what you have claimed within must show up externally—and living each moment as if it already has.

Ask yourself: *What frequency am I holding right now? Is it the static of doubt or the clear channel of "already done"?*

Choose wisely. Because life can only echo back what you broadcast.

7

The Effortless Thought

THERE IS A GREAT irony in the process of manifestation: the harder we try, the further away the dream seems to drift. The moment we clutch, grip, and attempt to force reality into being, we feel the resistance rise in the body like a tide. Tightness in the chest, tension in the jaw, restless thoughts circling over and over again—these are all signs that we are attempting to make happen what is already ours.

Manifestation was never meant to be born out of strain. The seed of a dream does not push against the soil in desperation; it simply grows, nurtured by the quiet forces of nature. In the same way, your desire is not asking you to wrestle it into being. It is asking you to allow it.

When we attempt to manifest with resistance, it feels heavy. We repeat affirmations but with doubt woven into the syllables. We visualize, but behind the vision sits the whisper, *what if it doesn't work?* We pray, we journal, we script, yet a part of us is still looking over our shoulder at the evidence of lack. That is not alignment. That is trying. And trying is effort with resistance braided into it.

Contrast that with the effortless thought—the kind that floats through your mind like a feather carried by a breeze. An effortless thought is light, natural, almost casual. It does not demand or strain. It simply declares, *of course it's mine.* It feels like truth, not possibility. It feels like memory, not hope. You don't have to repeat it a thousand times to make it stick; it already belongs to you.

The difference between resistance and effortless thought is the difference between rowing upstream until your arms ache and finally putting down the oars to discover the river has been carrying you all along. The effortless thought requires no wrestling, no negotiation, no justification. It is as natural as breathing.

How do we reach this effortlessness? First, we notice when resistance is present. Resistance often masquerades as productivity: the endless to-do lists, the relentless affirmations said with clenched teeth, the obsessive watching for signs.

If you can feel the tension, the strain, or the subtle panic beneath the surface, that is resistance. Recognize it, not as failure, but as feedback. Your body and your mind are telling you: *you are not relaxed in the knowing yet.*

Next, step back. Instead of asking, *how do I make this happen?* shift the question to *how do I allow this to feel natural?* Neville Goddard taught that the secret lies in feeling the wish fulfilled—but he added a key that many miss: *it must feel natural.* Not forced. Not like a performance. Natural, like slipping into a pair of shoes that were already made in your size and feel incredibly comfortable.

Third, practice the effortless thought itself. This is not about constructing elaborate sentences or repeating mantras until your throat is sore. It is about choosing simple, weightless declarations that feel obvious in your being. Thoughts like:
- *I love how natural this feels.*
- *This is just who I am now.*
- *I live here, in this reality, with ease.*

Then let those thoughts land, without grasping, without chasing. Just letting them be.

The effortless thought transforms manifestation from a desperate climb into a gentle exhale. It allows you to embody the truth that what you desire is already yours, not someday in the future, but now.

It's not about adding more force to your practices. It's about releasing the excess and returning to the simple, grounded knowing that the Universe is not asking you to fight. It is asking you to trust.

Thinking the effortless thought is like aligning yourself with a frequency that was always broadcasting: you simply tune in. Once you are tuned in, the evidence unfolds with startling ease. Opportunities appear. Conversations flow. Money arrives. The home, the love, the freedom, the health materialize, not because you fought for them, but because you *allowed* them.

This is the art of making a million look small: shifting from effort with resistance to effortless thought. When thought becomes natural, reality has no choice but to follow.

8

Stories That Make a Million Look Small

WE'VE TALKED ABOUT THE principle. You've seen glimpses of how it works in the examples we've explored, and perhaps you've even begun to imagine how it could unfold in your own life. Now let's ground it even further—with real stories of real people who truly made a million look small.

These aren't hypotheticals. These aren't metaphors. These are individuals who moved in alignment with their desire, took inspired action, and received results that would have once seemed unimaginable.

These stories are not just inspiring: they are proof that when belief is anchored and aligned with bold movement, the Universe responds. Often in ways that are faster, easier, and far more abundant than logic would ever allow.

These stories are not reserved for the lucky few. They are signposts for possibility. Let's walk through them one by one:

Amanda Hocking: The Self-Published Millionaire Author

Amanda Hocking was working a low-wage job and couldn't afford the publishing world's gatekeepers. But she believed in her stories, so she uploaded her books to Amazon's Kindle platform and priced them accessibly. What followed was nothing short of miraculous: millions of copies sold. In under two years, she made over $2 million in royalties—and went on to land a traditional publishing deal worth another $2 million. No big marketing team. No big advance. Just aligned belief, consistent inspired action, and openness to possibility.

Alex Tew: The Million-Dollar Homepage

A broke student with a million-dollar idea, Alex Tew wanted to fund his university education, so he launched a website—the Million Dollar Homepage—where he sold ad space one pixel at a time, $1 per pixel. It was odd. It was fresh. But it caught on. Media picked it up, companies bought in, and within months, he had sold all 1 million pixels. Revenue: $1 million. Proof that innovation + bold execution = limitless wealth.

Kanga Coolers: From Class Project to Multimillion Dollar Business

Born out of a class project at Clemson University, Kanga Coolers was created by a group of students who noticed a simple problem—people carrying around cold beer in warm boxes. Their solution? A koozie (that is, a fabric or foam sleeve designed to thermally insulate a beverage container) for your case. They entered and won a campus competition, refined the idea, and appeared on Shark Tank, where they landed a deal with Mark Cuban. Within a short span of time, their coolers generated millions in revenue. A simple idea. A willingness to play. And a total disregard for limits.

Robyn Fenty (Rihanna): A Billionaire Built from Belief

While known to most as a pop icon, Rihanna's massive wealth didn't only come from music—it came from her bold business moves. She cofounded Fenty Beauty with the mission to offer inclusive makeup to all skin tones, a space the industry had overlooked. Within weeks, the brand made $100 million. In a few short years, Rihanna became the wealthiest female musician in the world—not only from record sales, but from belief and vision extended into brand.

Daniel Ek: Spotify's Billion Dollar Symphony

Daniel Ek was a Swedish tech entrepreneur who had sold previous ventures for modest sums. But with Spotify, he didn't aim small. He believed he could change the way the world listened to music. He built the platform during the era of piracy, facing monumental industry resistance, but stayed true to the vision. Today Spotify is worth tens of billions, and Ek's personal net worth exceeds $2 billion. One idea. One commitment. Unshakable belief.

Sara Blakely: The Billionaire with $5,000 and a Pair of Scissors

She had no background in fashion. No investors. Just $5,000 and a problem she wanted to solve: panty lines. With a pair of scissors and a vision, she created the prototype for what would become Spanx. Sara Blakely became the youngest self-made female billionaire in the US—and she did it without outside funding. "I didn't know how it would happen," she said. "But I always believed it would."

Steve: The Art of Giving That Returned Millions

On a remote island in Fiji, an artist named Steve began giving away his paintings—not for marketing, but because he believed the energy of generosity would return to him multiplied. A year later, a wealthy art collector who had once received one of those pieces contacted him and offered $1.2 million for a private commission and full rights to his upcoming works. Proof that wealth doesn't always follow logic. But it always follows alignment.

Nathan Blecharczyk, Brian Chesky, and Joe Gebbia: The Airbnb Alchemy

Struggling to pay rent, these three roommates decided to rent out air mattresses in their living room during a conference weekend in San Francisco. They earned a few hundred dollars—but saw potential. That moment of inspired action led to the creation of Airbnb. In under a decade, it grew into a multibillion-dollar platform, transforming global travel. What began as desperation became domination. Because they dared to act.

Kylie Jenner: From Reality to Reality-Bending

Say what you will, but the numbers don't lie. At twenty-one years old, Kylie Jenner launched Kylie Cosmetics with a $250,000 investment from modeling gigs. Through savvy social media and direct-to-consumer sales, she crossed $1 billion in net worth within a few years. Was she visible? Yes. But she still had to believe. Had to create. Had to move. And she did.

Chris Guillebeau: The $100 Startup That Multiplied Millions

Author and entrepreneur Chris Guillebeau built an empire by showcasing stories of people who turned small investments into big wins. His own journey? He launched a blog, wrote a manifesto, and began offering guides for entrepreneurs—all without a giant platform or funding. His book, *The $100 Startup*, became a global best seller, generating millions in book sales, speaking engagements, and business growth. Proof that you can build big without starting big.

Lisa Price: Carol's Daughter and the Power of Homemade Wealth

Lisa Price started making natural beauty products in her kitchen, naming her creations Carol's Daughter in honor of her mother. She began selling them at flea markets and fairs, where her dedication to quality and her belief in the product built a community of loyal customers. Eventually, Carol's Daughter caught the attention of celebrities and investors—including Will Smith and Jada Pinkett Smith—and was later acquired by L'Oréal. From kitchen counter to corporate acquisition. It all started with belief.

Eric Yuan: Zooming Into Abundance

Eric Yuan was denied a U.S. visa multiple times. When he finally arrived, he worked at WebEx but believed video conferencing could be better. He left to build Zoom—quietly, steadily, with customer-first values. Within a few years, the platform exploded. When the pandemic hit, usage soared. Yuan's personal net worth jumped to over $15 billion. Alignment meets timing meets readiness.

Jaime Schmidt: Deodorant to Dollars

Jaime started making natural deodorant in her Portland kitchen. She had no experience in consumer products, but she had a desire: to offer something clean and effective. She sold at farmers markets, listened to feedback, and kept refining. Eventually, her brand—Schmidt's Naturals—was acquired by Unilever for a reported nine-figure sum. The initial investment? A few hundred dollars and a deep commitment.

The Breathwork Breakthrough

One of my clients built an entire million-dollar business by teaching people how to breathe. That's it. He focused on helping individuals reconnect with their breath through specific techniques that calmed the nervous system and expanded awareness. It may sound simple, but the demand was real—and so was the transformation his clients experienced. Through retreats, courses, and online programs, his aligned passion turned into prosperity.

The YouTube Prank Star Next Door

In our own neighborhood, there's a young man who earns millions annually by creating prank videos on YouTube. It may not be the path most would choose, but it's his. And it works for him, because he tapped into what made people laugh, built a loyal following, and turned views into dollars. The key isn't the content—it's the commitment. He chose his lane and owned it fully.

Young Millionaires from Stage: The Kids Who Did It

I remember presenting onstage at one of our live "Make a Million Look Small" events, delivering a keynote entirely focused on children—some under ten, some teenagers—who had made millions through ideas as varied as slime kits, YouTube toy reviews, or mobile apps. It was one of the most inspiring talks I've ever delivered. Because it proved, repeatedly, that when someone gets in harmony with the outcome—regardless of age, background, or experience—wealth is not only available but inevitable.

Each of these individuals made a million (or far more) look small. More importantly, they made the leap. Not all at once. Not always without fear. But they didn't wait for conditions to be perfect. They didn't overanalyze the *how*. They acted. They aligned. They trusted.

Let this chapter be more than inspiration: let it be evidence. If a million is possible for these enterprising individuals, it is not only possible for you—it's already seeking you.

The moment you stop treating a million as massive is the moment it starts arriving with ease.

9

Do What You Love and the Money Will Follow

THE PHRASE IS SWEET, isn't it? Almost like a song lyric, promising a life where passion and profit walk hand in hand. Yet I have seen far too many brilliant artists, soulful singers, eloquent writers, and deeply gifted healers who poured themselves into their art with love yet lived in scarcity. Their love was real, their dedication was deep, but money did not automatically follow. Why? Because love alone, while essential, is not enough.

To translate love into wealth, there must be knowledge: specialized, focused, marketable knowledge. You can have the most extraordinary book ever written sitting quietly on a shelf, but if no one knows it exists, it will gather dust while the world buys lesser works that are simply better promoted. Love is the fuel, but knowledge and strategy are the vehicle. Without a vehicle, love does not travel far in this material world.

I discovered this truth the hard way. When I wrote my first book, I was in a state of blissful ignorance. I was fueled by passion, by the love of writing, and by the desire to share something I believed could make a difference. I poured myself into that book with all my heart. I did not realize that writing the book is only a fraction of an author's responsibility. I have since heard a statistic—and I believe it—that only about 5 percent of an author's responsibility is writing and bringing their book to market: 95 percent of their success depends on marketing and promotion. At the time, I had no idea. I thought if you write a great book, people will simply find it. I thought love alone was enough.

But reality came quickly. I went almost broke writing a book on success. There was irony in that—crafting words on how to thrive while quietly wondering how I would pay the bills. My love for writing was real, but without knowledge of how to market, it left me in lack. For a moment, I felt my dream might collapse before it had even begun.

Yet there was one thing I had that pulled me forward: desire. A deep, unwavering desire to make this career a success. Desire compelled me to ask new questions. Desire pushed me to search for mentors. Desire gave me the courage to admit that I needed to learn a whole new skill set if I wanted to thrive.

That's when I was introduced to the world of online marketing. It was as if someone had handed me a set of keys to a door I hadn't even known existed. Once I began to study and master these strategies, everything shifted. I remember launching my first online campaign after learning this specialized knowledge. To my amazement, it brought in $43,500 in new revenue in a forty-eight-hour period. That number pleasantly surprised me. I had never seen anything like it before. And the best part? I quickly realized it wasn't just a one-time miracle. I could repeat it. I had found a pattern—a formula I could use again and again.

Over the years, I went on to run campaign after campaign, and the results continued to grow. I've hosted two-hour webinars that generated $279,000 in new revenue. I've held weekend events that brought in $1.1 million. And when I look at my body of work across the years, the numbers have reached into the eight figures.

I share this not to boast, but to illustrate a truth that changed everything for me: once you have the right knowledge and you apply it with consistency, the opportunities multiply. What happened for me can happen for anyone. The door that opened for me is open for you too. The same principles, the same strategies, and the same alignment that created those results are available to anyone who chooses to step through and use them.

From my first online marketing campaign, I leaned fully into mastering this skill. What began as a single campaign became a replicable system that ultimately generated millions of dollars in revenue over the years. That was the turning point: the moment I went from hoping that love alone would carry me to understanding that love plus specialized knowledge creates unstoppable momentum.

This is why I know, without question, that doing what you love is not enough on its own. Love is the seed. Desire is the fuel. But specialized knowledge—especially in marketing—allows that seed to flourish. When you combine all three, you create the synergy where your work is both deeply fulfilling and richly rewarded.

Doing what you love plants the seed. Learning how to prosper nurtures it. Together, they enable you to harvest a life of both fulfillment and abundance. Without one, the other struggles.

Love without knowledge may leave you in a state of longing. Knowledge without love may feel empty. But together, they create a beautiful harmony where your life becomes the living proof that passion and prosperity can indeed walk side by side.

Love ignites your passion, but specialized knowledge—especially in marketing—transforms it into prosperity. Do what you love, and learn what you must, so the money has a path to follow.

10

The Secret Key of Worthiness

WORTHINESS IS ONE OF those quiet forces that shapes every outcome in our lives, often without us even realizing it. It is the invisible yes or no that sits behind our dreams, answering the question of whether we will allow ourselves to receive what we say we want.

You can study manifestation, practice affirmations, visualize with intensity, and even take bold action—but if, in the deepest layers of your being, you carry the belief that you are not worthy, you will push away the very things you are calling toward you.

Worthiness does not always announce itself with loud declarations of self-doubt. It shows up in subtler, sneaky ways. It hides behind hesitation. It whispers in the urge to delay. It masks itself as "practicality" or "realism." Yet at its core, worthiness is simply this: the inner permission slip to receive what is already yours.

Like many of us, I learned this lesson in layers. From a very young age, I never doubted my worthiness when it came to earning money. I was drawn to earning, creating, and increasing my wealth, and I felt fully deserving of the rewards of my efforts.

In regard to love, I carried a different story. For many years, I did not feel fully worthy of a great partnership, of a love that would see and cherish me for exactly who I was. I went from relationship to relationship, I searched, I wondered if I was somehow lacking the qualities that would attract the man I longed for. It wasn't until I began to shift my internal beliefs and decided that I was worthy of the love I desired that everything changed.

When I finally aligned with the knowing that I was enough, that I was lovable exactly as I was, Denis walked into my life. He was, and is, the most wonderful man, and I can say with complete certainty that his arrival was a mirror of the worthiness I had finally claimed for myself. The love had always been waiting; it was my belief in worthiness that opened the door.

Worthiness doesn't just show up in love. It follows us into every arena where we stretch ourselves. I remember a time, years later, when I was about to step onto a large stage to speak before an audience. By that point, I had written books, coached clients around the world, and spoken many times before—but in that particular moment, as I waited backstage, a surge of doubt rose up like a wave. *Who am I to be here?* I thought. *Do I really belong on this stage, next to these other polished, seasoned speakers?*

That creeping voice of unworthiness nearly unraveled me in seconds. I had to stop and speak to myself with conviction. I reminded myself that while I might not deliver in the exact same style as others, my message was valuable, my experience was hard-won, and my heart was aligned with serving. I was worthy of that stage. The moment I owned that, I walked out and delivered what I came to share.

This experience taught me that even after years of growth, worthiness is not a one-time decision: it is something we claim repeatedly each time we expand into new levels of our lives.

Worthiness is one of the greatest silent barriers people face in regard to wealth. You might notice it when someone undercharges for their services, not because their work is not valuable, but because deep down they don't feel they're worth more. Or when someone hesitates to invest in themselves, even when the opportunity is exactly what they've been asking for, because a part of them does not believe they deserve the return. Or when money flows in—sometimes in abundance—but quickly flows out again, because the person does not feel worthy of keeping wealth.

Worthiness determines not only what we attract, but what we allow ourselves to hold. It is not enough to desire abundance: you must also feel worthy of it, or it will slip away like water through open fingers.

Worthiness is not something you earn or prove. It is not a reward for good behavior or for checking all the right boxes. Worthiness is inherent. It is given by the very fact that you are alive, breathing, and here. You are worthy because you exist. Period.

The work, then, is not about striving to become worthy: it is about unlearning the lies that ever made you believe you weren't worthy and knowing in your soul that you are worthy of everything you desire.

When worthiness feels far away, there are ways to reclaim this knowing. One simple but powerful practice is to stand before a mirror, look yourself in the eye, and declare, *I am worthy of this desire.*

At first it may feel awkward, even hollow, but repeated consistently, it begins to carve new grooves in your mind.

Another approach is to keep an evidence journal. Write down every moment when your desires, small or large, found their way to you. Let it remind you that the Universe has never failed to deliver—and that you have always been worthy of receiving.

Perhaps most important is identity work: consciously choosing to remember that you are not less than anyone else. You are not behind. You are not disqualified. You are not an exception to the laws of abundance.

The truth is, everything you desire has already been assigned to you by virtue of your existence. You don't need to justify it, you don't need to earn it, you don't need to prove yourself first. You *are* worthy, and your worthiness is unconditional. When you embrace this truth, doors swing wide open, and the flow of love, money, opportunities, and joy moves freely into your life.

A million looks small when you know you are worthy of more.

11

Your Relationship with Money

MONEY IS NOT JUST currency. It is energy. It is alive in the sense that it responds to you—to your attitude, your beliefs, and the way you feel about it. Your relationship with money is every bit as real as the relationship you have with a person. If you treat it with resentment, suspicion, or envy, it will remain elusive. If you treat it with gratitude, appreciation, and respect, it will flow into your life and continue to flow.

I have often heard people say, "It must be easy for them: they have so much money." On the surface, that sounds like a harmless observation, but underneath it carries a dangerous current of envy. Envy, as Bob Proctor reminded us many times, is ignorance of the law of abundance. Envy affirms lack. It affirms separation. It sends the message, "They have it, and I cannot." By declaring that, you push away the very thing you long to welcome.

Gratitude, however, is magnetic. Gratitude for what you already have. Gratitude for what others have. Gratitude even for the wealth you cannot yet see with your eyes, but which you know is being claimed in consciousness. When you celebrate another's success instead of resenting it, you are affirming the truth that abundance is not limited. You are saying to the Universe, "I see what is possible, and I welcome it into my own life."

I remember hearing bestselling author Wayne Dyer share a practice that stayed with me for life. He said that if he found a coin on the street—even something as small as ten cents—he would pause, pick it up, and say, "Thank you, Universe, for this example of abundance." To him, every small sign of wealth was worthy of appreciation. That struck me deeply. Gratitude is not reserved for windfalls or millions in the bank. It begins in the smallest details: clean water to drink, a bed to sleep in, food on the table, or even the discovery of a coin on the sidewalk.

This lesson of appreciation also came to me through the stories my father told of his own childhood. He grew up in poverty so deep that he often went hungry. Bread and milk were delivered by truck to the neighborhood, and he confessed that as a boy he would wait until the deliveryman carried food to a doorstep, then sneak onto the truck and steal a loaf of bread just so he had something to eat. He never slept on a real mattress. Instead, he filled a garbage bag with rags to cushion the floor beneath him.

Later, as a man with a family of his own, he was always grateful to be able to provide food for us. That gratitude never left him. His stories impressed on me the importance of appreciating the simplest things, not as ordinary, but as sacred. To this day, I give thanks for my bed, for warm water, for the smallest and the largest blessings. Gratitude expands everything it touches.

Think of money as a guest in your home. If you constantly criticize it, fear it, or resent it, will it want to stay? If you complain about bills, dread expenses, or obsess over lack, you are showing money the door. But if you welcome it warmly, treat it with honor, use it joyfully, and express appreciation for it, then money feels at home with you. It doesn't just visit: it lingers, and it brings its friends.

You may think I'm suggesting money has feelings of its own. It doesn't. Money is energy, and so are you. The way you *feel* about money—the vibration you hold when you think about it, speak about it, or use it—determines whether it flows easily or resists you. Like energy attracts like energy, so when you're aligned with appreciation, ease, and openness, money responds in kind.

Your relationship with money is revealed in small, everyday interactions. Do you celebrate paying your bills as a sign of your ability to exchange value, or do you resent them as a drain? Do you feel joy when others prosper, or do you compare and shrink? Do you receive gifts and opportunities with ease, or do you push them away with guilt, self-doubt, or the subtle belief that you are unworthy? Every one of these moments is a conversation with money. And like in any relationship, money listens to how it is being treated.

Wealth is not only about numbers on a balance sheet. It is about energy, harmony, and flow. When you learn to love money as an ally rather than fearing it as an enemy, you create an atmosphere where it feels at home with you. That is when it multiplies and expands. That is when your bank account begins to mirror the love, respect, and gratitude you have chosen to extend.

Your relationship with money determines how it shows up in your life. Envy repels it. Gratitude multiplies it. Treat money as a welcome guest, and it will always feel at home with you.

12

Fear as Fuel

THE MOMENT YOU ENTERTAIN a new idea of something you would truly love, like having millions in the bank or owning a beautiful waterfront home, your old conditioning often reveals itself in protest. The beliefs that have been firmly impressed in your subconscious mind begin to push back, because the new thought is not yet in harmony with the patterns by which you've lived until now. That resistance frequently shows up as fear.

Fear shows up the moment you stretch beyond what you already know. That's not weakness. That's not failure. That's not a sign that you should turn back. It's evidence that you are in the presence of growth.

If you were only ever doing what you already knew how to do, you would never feel fear. Familiar actions don't activate fear, because they don't stretch you. But when you reach for more—for the dream home, the financial leap, the bold career move, the decision that makes your stomach tighten—fear shows up. Not because you're wrong, but because you're right on track.

Fear is not a stop sign. It is a signal. It's the flashing light that says: *Pay attention. You are expanding. This is your opportunity for growth.*

Fear and faith are opposite frequencies. If you're in fear, you're not in alignment with your desire. If you're in faith, you're living in the vibration of the outcome already fulfilled. You can't hold them both at the same time. You get to choose.

Fear can be seen as an acronym for *false evidence appearing real*. It's the story your old conditioning tells you: *You can't. You'll fail. You don't deserve it. Who do you think you are?*

Faith, on the other hand, is living from the awareness that what you want is already here. Faith is choosing to believe in the unseen. Faith is aligning with the end result as though it's a memory instead of a wish.

In 1995, I bought a home without having the money to pay for it. The decision filled me with fear. My mind ran wild with what-ifs. My body was gripped with tension. I lay awake at night wondering what I had done.

Then I recognized that fear was simply a signal: a flashing light saying I was moving into new territory. I realized I had a choice: I could allow fear to consume me, or I could redirect that energy into faith.

I chose faith. I imagined the outcome as already done. I pictured myself walking through that house, enjoying it, celebrating life inside those walls. I let myself *feel* the joy of ownership. That shift dissolved the fear and ignited faith. And when faith leads, solutions unfold.

Faith, like a muscle, is built through use. At first it may feel shaky, unsteady, even uncertain, just as a beginner in the gym struggles with a new weight. But every time you redirect fear into faith—every time you choose to imagine the outcome as already done, to speak the words of certainty, to act in alignment—you are strengthening that muscle.

Over time, those repetitions accumulate. The belief that once felt fragile begins to feel natural. The doubt that once shouted becomes only a whisper. Gradually, almost without noticing, you find yourself standing taller, anchored in a faith that feels unshakable because you have practiced it into being.

Just as this practice strengthens us on a personal level, history is full of examples of people who built their dreams by choosing faith over fear, even when the stakes were enormous. Every great leap carries fear. Long before he became known for buying the Dallas Cowboys, Jerry Jones borrowed $800,000 to invest in an oil well. It was a bold move at a time when he was already carrying heavy debt, but that well produced $100 million in revenue. Imagine if fear had stopped him. Risk and fear travel together, but those who succeed don't allow fear to drive. They let it ride along in the passenger seat while faith takes the wheel.

I've seen this truth with my clients too. When they set bold goals, fear shows up immediately: *What if I fail? What if people laugh at me? What if I lose everything?* But the moment they reframe that fear—*What if it works? What if I'm supported? What if it's already mine?*—the fear loses its grip. Suddenly they step into action, and action, aligned with faith, produces results.

Every time I've launched a new program, signed a book contract, or stood on a stage in front of hundreds, fear has been right there. My heart races. My palms sweat. My mind offers every reason to back away. But instead of retreating, I've learned to interpret those feelings differently. That rush of energy isn't proof I'm in danger. It's proof I'm alive, growing, stretching into new territory.

Think of an athlete at the starting line of a Olympics contest. Do you think they're calm, cool, and fearless? Not at all. Their heart is pounding. Their body is buzzing with adrenaline. But they don't call it fear. They call it readiness. They've trained themselves to interpret the sensation of fear as fuel for performance.

You can do the same. The energy of fear can be transmuted into focus, determination, and courage. It's the same energy: the only difference is the meaning you assign to it.

When fear shows up, don't run. Don't collapse. Don't judge yourself for it. Instead, try this:

Recognize the signal. Say to yourself: *This is fear. That means I'm growing.*

Reframe the story. Ask, *what if this is already done? What if everything works out?*

Redirect the energy. Use the nervous energy as fuel. Take one bold step forward while you're in this heightened state: send the email, make the call, write the first page.

Choose faith. Close your eyes and feel your goal as complete. Invite yourself into the vibration of it already accomplished.

Fear will visit whenever you're standing on the edge of transformation. That doesn't mean you're in the wrong place. It means you're exactly where you need to be.

The next time fear rises up, don't see it as your enemy. See it as proof that you're expanding, that you're on the edge of becoming more, that you're stepping into the dream that once felt too big to imagine. Celebrate that moment, because celebration shifts the energy. It transforms fear into fuel, turning what once felt heavy into a signal that you are exactly where you're meant to be.

Fear doesn't have to stop you. It doesn't have to shrink you. Fear can fuel you. When you learn to transmute fear into faith, you'll discover that the very energy that once tried to hold you back can become the fire that propels you forward.

13

The Questions That Make a Million Look Small

QUESTIONS SHAPE EVERYTHING. THE questions you ask determine the answers you receive, the state you live in, and the results you create. Every question is like a spotlight, and wherever you aim it, your energy flows. Ask small, limiting questions, and you will get small, limiting answers. Ask expansive, aligned questions, and you position yourself on the frequency where possibility becomes inevitable.

There are destructive questions. They drag you down with their very phrasing. *Why can't I ever get ahead? Why does this always happen to me? What if I fail?* These are not harmless. They are instructions to your mind, and the mind will obey, finding proof for why things don't work, why money is scarce, why success is elusive. These kinds of questions are like doors closing, shutting you off from the abundance you seek.

There are gentler questions. *How will I move forward today? What could I do to feel a little better right now?* These questions nudge you, step by step, in the right direction. They're like walking up the stairs—steady and useful, but slow.

Then there are the alignment questions: the ones that bypass fear, doubt, and hesitation altogether and drop you straight into the vibration of your desire fulfilled. These are the express elevator to the top. No stops. No delays. Just immediate alignment. They don't make money seem bigger. They make millions look small. A perfect example of an alignment question is asking yourself: *Now that my dream is fulfilled, how do I feel?*

One of my favorite questions is only four words: *what would I love?* Ask it when you're uncertain. Ask it when you feel fear. Ask it when you're staring at a decision and don't know which way to turn. Ask it when you've been caught in negative energy. It works every single time.

What would I love? pulls you out of lack and into desire. It stops you from asking what you can afford, what seems reasonable, or what others expect of you. Those are the small, constricting questions that keep you stuck. *What would I love?* is expansive. It is the language of the soul. When you live from that place, wealth arrives as an outcome of alignment, not an obstacle to it.

I remember one vacation down south, strolling with my husband on a sunny afternoon. We passed a villa with a "For Sale" sign. I stopped in my tracks. My husband looked at me curiously and asked what I was doing. I pointed to the sign. He shrugged and said, "So?" I smiled and said, "It's for sale. Wouldn't it be wonderful to have a home down south to escape to during those cold winter months?" In that moment, my vibration shifted. That single question opened the door to a new possibility. It wasn't about logic or affordability. It was about desire.

That desire didn't stay a daydream. That very night, I made the decision—not someday, not later, but now. I bought the villa, put the deal in motion, and sixty days later, I closed on it, paid in full with cash. The way appeared because I aligned with the decision. I ended up launching a new program online during that time, and it generated every dollar I needed. The lesson? The way was always there, waiting on me. The moment I became clear, the funds flowed.

Bob Proctor used to say that when you see something that excites or intrigues you, ask, *do I want it?* If the answer is yes, don't shut it down. Let yourself entertain the idea of having it. Because in the asking, you shrink the size of the dream. What looked enormous becomes accessible. That's how a million begins to look small.

That's what questions do: they either close doors or open them. Destructive questions slam them shut. Gentle questions crack them open. But expansive questions like *what would I love?* throw them wide open, letting the light pour in.

Here's what makes these questions even more powerful: "why" questions. Neuroscientist Andrew Huberman has explained how the brain can't resist closing loops. A *why* question is like an unfinished puzzle that your brain must solve. Ask, *why do things always work out for me? Why is money flowing to me so easily now? Why am I so aligned with abundance?* and your brain will go searching for proof. It's not wishful thinking. It's biology. Your brain scans for evidence that matches the question, and in doing so, it strengthens those beliefs.

I've seen this work time and time again. When I've been afraid to take a leap, a single question has flipped the switch: *what would I love?* Instantly my energy shifts from fear to faith, from contraction to expansion. When clients have been stuck, I've guided them into asking, *why is it so easy for me to succeed?* or *why do I always attract the right opportunities?* I've watched their entire state transform before my eyes. In those moments, the "impossible" amounts of money they once imagined suddenly looked small, because they were standing in the vibration of already having it.

This is how you make a million look small. If you ask, *how can I just scrape by?* you'll live in scraping by. If you ask, *what would I love?* you move into a new realm where a million is not the goal but the beginning: the floor, not the ceiling. The real goal is the life you would love—the freedom, the experiences, the joy, the impact. The money is simply the tool.

When fear shows up, don't ask, *what if I fail?* Ask instead, *what would I love?* When doubt creeps in, don't ask, *why can't I?* Ask instead, *why is it so easy for me now?* These are not idle affirmations. They are activations. They engage your mind, align your vibration, and set the law of attraction into motion.

Every question is an invitation. You can invite lack, or you can invite abundance. You can invite fear, or you can invite faith. You can invite limitation, or you can invite possibility. The choice is always yours.

When you choose the right questions, the ones that elevate and expand, millions no longer look overwhelming or impossible. They look small, because your vision is so much larger.

14

Reduce It to the Ridiculous

THE VIEW FROM THE top is always clearer. When you climb a mountain, the rocks that once felt like obstacles under your boots shrink into specks in the landscape. From above, the twists and turns of the trail make sense in a way they never could while you were gasping for breath on the climb.

The same principle applies to your goals. When you stretch your thinking far above what you *think* you want, suddenly what once looked massive begins to appear small—even ridiculous.

This is not just a trick of perspective; it's a universal law. The law of polarity tells us that everything exists in relation to its opposite. Hot only makes sense in contrast to cold. Up is only meaningful because down exists. Big only has significance when placed against something small. Without contrast, there is no definition, no meaning.

Think about the rooms of a house. A closet feels small in comparison to a bedroom. A bedroom may feel small compared to a ballroom in a hotel. A ballroom may feel small compared to a stadium. The point is: size, scale, and significance are never absolute: they are relative. So is your million.

When you look at $1 million from the vantage point of someone struggling to pay their bills, it feels monumental, almost untouchable. But when you deliberately place that same million against a larger figure—$10 million, $50 million, $100 million—it suddenly shrinks in perspective.

That's the beauty of *reducing it to the ridiculous.* It's not about dismissing the dream. It's about changing its relationship to something bigger so that your nervous system relaxes, your imagination expands, and your faith begins to soar.

I've done this exercise with clients countless times. One of my favorite assignments was asking them to create a $100 million plan, not because they necessarily wanted or needed that amount, but because the act of stretching their imagination that far liberated them from the fear of smaller goals.

At first, they would resist. "Peggy, I can't even imagine a million. How could I possibly map out a hundred million?" But as they played with it, sketched ideas, and dared to think bigger, something magical happened: the fear dissolved. They saw how ridiculous it was to fear $1 million when they had just mapped out $100 million.

When you reduce it to the ridiculous, you are using the law of relativity to your advantage. Instead of letting your mind shrink a goal into impossibility, you stretch it so far that the original goal becomes light, obvious, inevitable.

Let's play with some numbers. Suppose you want to make $1 million. That number may feel heavy at first, so let's blow it up. What about $10 million? How could you imagine doing that?

Maybe you create a $1,000 program and sell it to 10,000 people. That's $10 million.

Maybe you start a membership community with two tiers: one at $50 per month, one at $100 per month. With 5,000 members in each tier, you're bringing in $750,000 a month. That's $9 million in a year, and just a little more growth takes you to $10 million.

Maybe you sell a book and earn $5 in royalties per copy. A million copies sold is $5 million. Two million copies? Ten million.

These are not fanciful scenarios. They're simply possibilities. When you open your mind to what is possible, you loosen the grip of fear. You stop asking, *can I?* and you begin asking, *which way would I love?* In that single shift, doubt loses its hold and creativity takes the driver's seat.

This principle works outside of money too. Consider relationships. Someone may feel devastated by a breakup because their mind has collapsed the entire world into that one bond. But when they place their life into a larger context—friendships, family, new opportunities, even the infinite potential of meeting someone more aligned with them—the relationship that once looked like the whole world begins to shrink in perspective. This act doesn't erase the feelings, but it reframes them. That's the same energy you bring when you "reduce it to the ridiculous" in pursuit of your goals.

Every great teacher in this field has reminded us that your perspective creates your experience. Bob Proctor often told me that if you want to earn more money, don't lower the bar to what you think is reasonable: raise your vision until the "reasonable" becomes laughable. Neville Goddard spoke of feeling the wish fulfilled so naturally that anything less than the desired outcome begins to feel absurd. They were all teaching the same principle: magnify your thinking so that your fear loses its scale.

When you play with $10 million, $50 million, $100 million, the $1 million that once felt impossible becomes something you can hold in your hands without trembling. You no longer approach it with desperation or intimidation. You approach it with certainty, because in comparison, it's small.

Ask yourself: what if $1 million isn't big at all? What if it only looks that way because of your vantage point? Climb higher. Stretch your imagination. Place that million against something grander. Reduce it to the ridiculous. And watch how quickly the dream that once scared you begins to feel like the most natural thing in the world.

15

The Most Precious Commodity

MONEY CAN BE LOST and regained. Fortunes can come and go. But time is a one-way street, and once a moment is spent, it is gone forever. We tend to guard our money, yet most people spend their time as if it were limitless. It is not. The way you treat time will determine whether millions look like a mountain you could never climb or whether they shrink into something small, attainable, and natural.

When I was diagnosed with metastatic cancer at the age of sixty-two, I faced the reality that my time on this earth might be cut short. Even though I was already living a life on purpose, the experience cracked me open to a deeper realization: time is more precious than anything else I could ever hold. This diagnosis gave me a kind of clarity that only comes when you are confronted with the fragility of life. From that point forward, I decided that I would no longer invest my time with people who drained me, nor would I invest my time doing things that didn't bring joy, meaning, or alignment. Life is too short to waste.

Today I am grateful to say that I am 100 percent healthy. The cancer is completely gone. I used my mind every single day to support my healing, while also following the wisdom and guidance of my oncologists and medical team. It was alignment in action: body, mind, and spirit working together. And just as I teach in every other area of life, I learned again that the same principles apply: belief, imagination, and faith shape outcomes.

I remember a conversation with Bob Proctor when he was in his eighties. He said, "At this age, you realize how precious your time left on earth is. I choose to only invest time with people I enjoy." I'll never forget that. Here was a man who had influenced millions around the world, and yet what mattered most to him in his later years was the *quality* of his time and whom he shared it with. I felt so grateful to be one of those people he chose. His words reinforced what my cancer diagnosis had already taught me: time is the most valuable commodity we have, and how we spend it defines the quality of our lives.

Most people misuse their time without realizing it. They spend hours overexplaining themselves to people who will never be convinced. They procrastinate on the things that matter most. They say yes to obligations out of guilt instead of alignment. They confuse being busy with being productive, and in doing so, they squander their most precious resource. Then they wonder why their dreams feel far away, why $1 million feels unattainable, why their goals always seem to be slipping out of reach. It's because the way you use your time determines the vibration you live in. Wasted time keeps you out of alignment.

When you decide to master your time, everything changes. Time must serve your vision, not the other way around. It is about deliberately carving out space for what keeps you aligned: your imagination, your journaling, your visioning, your creative work. It means guarding your attention, because every moment given to the meaningless is taken from the meaningful.

This is why mentors matter so much. Working with someone who has already achieved what you want to achieve compresses years into months. Bob was that mentor for me, and his guidance saved me decades of wandering down blind alleys. Most importantly, he showed me how to get the results I desired.

When you spend your time with people who stretch your thinking, you collapse the gap between where you are and where you want to be. It makes millions look small, because you've gone directly to the source. Compare that to spending years trying to figure it all out on your own—wasting the one thing you can never get back.

Time is a higher form of currency than money. Money is flexible, renewable, replaceable. Time is finite, and it only moves in one direction. When you begin to treat time as your highest form of currency, money begins to flow more freely. Why? Because you are no longer wasting your hours on things that shrink you. You are investing your time in things that expand you. You are living in the frequency of the outcome, not in the waiting room of "someday." That energy compounds, and suddenly millions no longer look like mountains: they look inevitable.

When someone is truly aligned with their goals—whether it's having millions in the bank, owning the dream home, or living with complete financial freedom—they are not waiting for it to happen someday. They are *feeling it now*. Not later, not next month, not "when everything works out," but right now. That is true alignment. It's a present-tense reality in your imagination and in your emotions.

This is why frustration over timing is always a signal that alignment has slipped. People sabotage themselves when they start asking, *when is this going to happen?* That question comes from lack and impatience, and it pushes the very thing they want further away.

When you are living in the energy of "already done," time becomes irrelevant. You don't need to know *when*, because you are already living the frequency of the outcome.

In fact, when you stop obsessing over timing, everything tends to speed up. Time bends for those who live in alignment. What looked like it would take ten years can collapse into one. What looked like it would take months can happen in a day. The secret is to live the feeling now, and trust that time will reorganize itself around your alignment.

My cancer diagnosis gave me the clarity to treat time as precious, but you don't need to wait for a crisis to make the same decision. You can choose right now to treat your time as sacred. Audit where your hours are going. Cut what doesn't align. Double down on what does. Millions look small to those who treat every moment as sacred. The way you use your time will either keep you waiting for your dream life or move you directly into it. Time is the currency that makes all the difference.

16

The Power of Persistence

THERE'S A MOMENT IN every journey when quitting feels like the logical choice. When the evidence is thin, the silence is deafening, and the dream starts to flicker like a candle caught in the wind. In those very moments, you must access the muscle of persistence. If you don't hold tight like a dog with a bone, you might as well pack it in.

I learned that lesson early in my journey as an author. Before the best sellers, before the stages, before the audiences and accolades, there were days of doubt. There were closed doors. There were polite "no, thank yous" and long stretches of nothing.

But I was stubborn in my belief. It was not the kind of stubbornness born from ego, but from vision. From a fire that refused to die, no matter how many buckets of "reality" were thrown its way.

I remember writing my book *Be a Dog with a Bone* not just as a title but as a lifeline. It was born from experience, from the lived understanding that you simply cannot release your dream because it hasn't arrived yet. That dream, that vision, is yours. You've been entrusted with it. If you give it up because the path feels slow or lonely or unclear, you're letting your dream die in your hands.

Let's talk about the word *lonely*. Pursuing a dream at this level can feel lonely at times, because most people don't think this way. Even the people who love you most may try to protect you with advice that is almost always filtered through their own limitations and beliefs. They mean well, but if you're not careful, their doubt can sound louder than your own faith. Sometimes you may even feel unsupported under your own roof.

But successful people keep going when there's no evidence in sight. They move forward even when the way isn't clear. They hold tight to the vision, knowing that the clarity, the resources, and the support will appear at the right time. Choosing persistence in those moments is choosing the path of every great achiever who has ever brought a dream to life.

Persistence is not about pushing blindly or working yourself into the ground. It's about commitment. It's about returning (once again) to the energy of completion, even when your outer world hasn't caught up. It's waking up and choosing to believe before the evidence appears. It's holding the vibration of *I know this is mine* when others shake their heads or raise their eyebrows.

Let me be clear: persistence doesn't mean you never feel like giving up. Everyone feels it. I've felt it. Phil Goldfine, my dear friend and Academy Award–winning producer, has felt it. I would even venture to say that Bob Proctor felt it at times too. The difference is not that we never encounter those moments; it's that we recognize them for what they are. Like fear, the urge to quit is not a sign of failure; it's a signal. It indicates that a belief is being stretched, that a new level of growth is being demanded. When I feel that inner resistance, I remind myself: this isn't weakness, this is opportunity. It's the chance to reinforce the belief, to double down on faith, to align more fully with the result I've already claimed.

The extra mile is empty. Most people give up. Most people won't stretch themselves. Most people would rather wait for proof than *become* the proof.

But you're not most people. You must be willing to do what others won't. To pick up the phone one more time. To walk into the room again. To speak your dream out loud even when it feels absurd.

The story "Three Feet from Gold" in *Think and Grow Rich* tells about two men who, after some success in gold prospecting, found that the vein of ore had disappeared. They continued searching but eventually gave up. They sold their equipment to a junk dealer, who consulted a mining engineer. The engineer discovered a fault line, which meant that a rich vein of gold was found just *three feet* from where the two men had stopped drilling.

The impact of that story has never left me. Many people are *this close*—and they stop. They stop because they can't see the end yet. But *lack of evidence is not evidence of lack*. Just because you can't see it with your eyes doesn't mean it's not real. The roots grow before the flower ever breaks the surface.

Persistence is spiritual. It's not just about effort; it's about alignment. It's about saying, "I *know* who I am and where I'm going" and walking in that truth even when the lights haven't turned green.

There will be people who question you. There will be days you question yourself. But when that moment comes—and it *will* come—dig your heels in. Be a dog with a bone. Hold it tight.

You're not just chasing a dream. You're becoming the kind of person who never lets go of what's already yours.

17

The Stream Must Flow

THERE IS A SACRED truth embedded in the essence of wealth: what flows, grows. Like water, money was never meant to stagnate. It is designed to move, to circulate, to serve, to bless. In that flow, in that motion of giving and receiving, lies the miracle of multiplication.

Too often, especially in the pursuit of financial abundance, people fall into a trap of hoarding. They clutch tightly to what they have, believing it must be protected at all costs. But the tighter the grip, the more we constrict the stream. The flow dries up, not because the source has run out, but because the channel is blocked by fear, scarcity, or the illusion of safety.

Let me be clear: I am all for investing wisely. I believe in creating a healthy net worth, in setting money aside for retirement, for future goals, for joyful expansion. But there is a distinct energetic difference between purposeful direction and fear-based withholding. Money hoarded out of fear carries a very different vibration than money allocated with clarity and vision.

There is certainly wisdom in investing and setting money aside for the future. The key is the energy behind it. Saving for joyful expansion, for a dream trip, or for a secure and abundant retirement feels entirely different from stockpiling out of fear. One is rooted in vision and growth; the other in lack and worry. The first multiplies; the second diminishes.

Bob Proctor used to say something that struck me to my core: "If you're saving for a rainy day, it means you're expecting one—and you'll likely get one." The energy behind that kind of saving is rooted in fear, in the expectation of misfortune. And what you expect, you attract.

Bob also told a story that I've never forgotten. When he was young, a man in his neighborhood passed away. After his death, the survivors discovered tens of thousands of dollars stuffed inside the walls of his home—money that had been hidden, unused, doing absolutely nothing. No joy. No circulation. No creation. Just hidden potential buried by fear. That's not prosperity. That's poverty disguised as prudence.

True wealth flows. It blesses others. It moves into causes, experiences, expansion, and delight. When you tip generously, you are saying to the Universe, "I trust the flow." When you invest in yourself or others, you're demonstrating your knowing that abundance is never in short supply.

The Universe does not reward stagnation. It rewards movement. Circulation is the signal that you trust in the stream. You don't need to hoard, because you understand the river runs wide and deep—and you have full access to it.

While circulation includes spending, there is another sacred aspect of wealth that is often overlooked: giving value.

Prosperity isn't just about what you receive: it's about what you give. When you solve problems, uplift others, or bring light to the world in any form, you're participating in the highest form of wealth creation. Value given is wealth invited. The more you pour into others with love, intention, and excellence, the more abundance will find its way back to you—pressed down and overflowing.

We are each richly rewarded in direct proportion to the value we provide. Not because of some transactional scorecard, but because the Universe always reflects who we are being. If you are being a light, a solution, a channel of goodness, it is impossible not to be blessed.

You want more wealth? Serve more deeply. Show up more powerfully. Bring your best to the world, even when no one is watching. Especially then.

So give. Invest. Circulate. Whether it's $10, $100, or $100,000. Be wise, but never scared. Let your money flow into good things and greater good. Let your service speak for you before your results ever do. In truth, you are not losing anything. You are expanding everything.

If you want to make a million look small, you must become a vessel of abundance—one who allows money to move with joy, gratitude, and ease. One who gives generously of their gifts and knows that the stream is endless. When you do, the Universe responds in kind. The stream never stops flowing for the one who flows with it.

18

The Gestation Period

THERE IS A NATURAL rhythm to all creation. No matter how clear the vision, how strong the desire, or how aligned the intention, there will always be a space between planting the seed and witnessing the bloom. This is not a delay. It is not a punishment. It is simply law.

In fact, it falls under the natural law of gender, which teaches that everything in creation has a gestation period. Just as there is a set time for seeds to sprout or babies to be born, every idea and desire must be given its season to develop. You cannot rush it, and you cannot skip it. The law of gender ensures that when the right conditions of faith and alignment are met, the birth of your dream is inevitable.

One of the most common misunderstandings about manifestation is the expectation of immediacy. We imagine a thing, we feel into it, we hold the vibration—and then we wonder why it hasn't yet appeared. But that's like planting a carrot seed and digging it up the next day, frustrated that it hasn't yet become a harvest. We know how long some things take. A carrot, a tomato, a pregnancy—we accept that these have gestational timelines.

But with desires like earning millions, publishing best sellers, healing relationships, or acquiring a dream home, we don't get a delivery estimate. So the mind gets anxious. The ego starts to interfere. We question the process. We question ourselves.

But I'll tell you this: if you're not seeing results, it's only one of two things: either you're not consistently aligned with the outcome, or the gestation period hasn't completed. That's it. That's the truth. If you are truly aligned and you remain there, your success is inevitable. It must happen. It cannot *not* happen. The law responds with precision.

The problem is that most people don't stay in alignment long enough. They jump in, then out. They believe, then doubt. They visualize, then react to what is. They play in the dream for a moment, then get pulled back into lack, fear, or impatience. It's not that the seed isn't good. It's that the gardener keeps digging it up.

Robert Collier said it beautifully in his book *The Secret of the Ages*: "It is not enough to know that you have this power; you must use it every hour of every day."

That quote has stayed with me for decades. It's a reminder that this isn't a one-time effort or an occasional alignment. This is a way of being.

In *The Moment of Alignment*, I described it as the precise moment when intention becomes reality. That moment is not when you see the evidence appear in your world. It's when you become the version of yourself who already has it. It's when you are so deeply saturated in the energy of completion that reality has no choice but to catch up. But—and this is important—you must stay there. You must *reside* in that state. Not visit it. Not flirt with it. You must live there.

Let's get practical for a moment. If I asked you to close your eyes and imagine that your million—or millions—are here right now, how would you feel? The honest answer might be something like calm. Grateful. Free. Relieved. Expanded. That's alignment. That's your evidence. That's your inner confirmation.

When you dwell in that energy throughout your day, moment to moment, you are radiating the frequency of fulfillment. That is your job. Not to guess how long it will take. Not to worry if it's working. But to live in the frequency that it is already done.

Manifestation doesn't take time: it takes alignment. Alignment, held consistently over time, reveals the form. If you're truly living in the knowing that your desire is yours, you will feel no urgency, no grasping, no panic.

You will feel peace. And that peace is the birthplace of miracles. You may not know *when*. But you can know *that*. That it is done. That it is yours. That it has arrived through the beautiful, lawful, perfect unfolding of time.

So if you're wondering how long it takes to make a million look small, the answer is simple: it takes exactly as long as it takes for you to remain aligned in the truth that it is already yours—and to hold that alignment with the quiet, powerful certainty of someone who knows how this all works.

Keep watering the seed. Keep tending the field. Stay in the vibration of the result. And trust the divine timing that is always, always on your side.

19

The Calm of Completion

THERE IS A SACRED power in relaxation. Not the kind of relaxation that comes from slipping into a warm bath or reclining in a chair (though those can be lovely), but the relaxation that comes from surrendering the internal battle. The relaxation that arises when you drop the frantic need to figure it all out, to control every detail, and instead rest in the quiet certainty that it is already done.

Most people live in tension. Their bodies are tight, their minds restless, their words hurried. They chase outcomes like a runner gasping for air, trying to force life into cooperation. They don't realize that tension is a signal of disbelief. Tension says, "I don't trust this process. I'm afraid it won't work out. I must keep pushing." And the Universe, ever faithful, reflects back that state of struggle with delayed results and frustrating obstacles.

Relaxation, by contrast, is the language of faith. It is a posture of knowing. It is the calm of someone who doesn't need to see evidence, because the evidence already lives within them. It is the serenity of a soul that whispers, *"This is mine. This is done. I appreciate it. I simply choose to live it."* When you relax into the knowing, you are no longer chasing the dream, you are embodying it. And embodiment magnetizes.

Think about it this way: the most natural parts of your life right now—your home, your car, your relationships—don't cause you tension. You don't wake up in the morning wondering if your bed will still be yours. You don't fret over whether your car will be parked outside, waiting for you. You don't sit down at your dinner table anxious about whether you belong there. These things feel natural, normal, unquestioned. Because they are unquestioned, they remain stable in your life.

That is exactly how your desires must feel. The more natural they become in your inner world, the more inevitable they become in your outer world. Relaxation is the bridge between imagining and possessing. It takes your dream from being an anxious hope to being a calm certainty. The frantic vibration of "will it happen?" dissolves into the steady hum of "it already has."

This is why I tell my clients, over and over again: *relax in the knowing*. The desire is already complete in the invisible. The seed has been planted. The soil is rich. The growth is underway. Anxiety only digs up the roots, disrupting what is naturally unfolding. Relaxation allows the process to mature.

The paradigms, of course, will protest. They will surface with their old noise, insisting that nothing is happening, warning you of failure, tempting you to panic. That is their role—old conditioning doing its best to survive. But the more you practice the naturalness of completion, the less persuasive that battle becomes. The fear voice may still knock, but it will no longer feel like the master. You will recognize it for what it is: an echo of an old identity you no longer inhabit.

Here's the beautiful truth: when you learn to relax in the knowing, life surprises you. The *how* reveals itself in ways you never could have orchestrated. When you are relaxed, you are open. You can see opportunities that tension would have blinded you to. You can receive inspiration without resistance. You can let the path unfold instead of strangling it with impatience.

Relaxation is not passivity. It doesn't mean sitting on the couch waiting for a miracle to land in your lap. Relaxation means you are anchored in faith as you move through your day. You make the phone call. You send the email. You put in the offer. You take inspired action, but you do it from a place of calm inevitability, not frantic desperation. You act as though it is already yours, because in truth, it is.

Let this be your daily atmosphere: unclench your jaw, soften your shoulders, slow your breath, and remember who you are. You are the one who already has it. You are the one living in the dream fulfilled. Every action you take, every thought you think, every word you speak can arise from that steady center of knowing.

On the wall of my own office, I have a single word framed in bold letters: *RELAX*. It is not a decoration. It is a command. It is the essence of creation itself. For when you relax in the knowing, the struggle ends, the resistance dissolves, and the current of life carries you effortlessly into the visible completion of what you already hold in the unseen.

Breathe in certainty. Breathe in gratitude. Let this rhythm steady you. Let it remind you that everything you desire is not on its way—it is here, now, fully alive within you. When you live in that calm truth, the world has no choice but to conform.

20

The Currency of Imagination

IMAGINATION IS NOT CHILD's play. It is the most powerful and valuable currency you possess. Long before money ever enters your account, long before keys are handed over, long before any physical evidence appears, imagination is the medium of exchange through which all creation flows.

Most of us, however, were trained out of using it. As children, we were told to "pay attention," "stop daydreaming," or "be realistic." In classrooms of thirty or more, a teacher's role was not to encourage wild visions but to maintain order, and any child caught gazing out the window was quickly corrected.

Parents and caregivers, often well-meaning, dismissed big dreams as silly or impossible. Over time, those repeated corrections left their mark: many grew up believing that imagination was frivolous, even dangerous. So by the time we reached adulthood, the faculty that was designed to build worlds had been muted. The tragedy is not that children dream, but that too many adults stop.

Every invention, every masterpiece, every breakthrough the world has ever celebrated began as nothing more than a picture in someone's mind. Airplanes, symphonies, skyscrapers, books, businesses—all of them were once invisible visions before they became undeniable realities. The people who brought them forth did not treat imagination as fantasy. They treated it as fact-in-waiting. They invested in it as a banker invests in gold.

When you use your imagination deliberately, you are writing checks from the account of the unseen. You are placing your order with the Universe, not with words alone, but with feeling and vivid imagery. The more clearly you imagine, the more certain you feel, the richer your investment. And here's the miracle: unlike money, imagination never runs out. The more you spend it, the more it multiplies.

Yet most people misuse imagination. Instead of creating futures, they rehearse fears. They picture worst-case scenarios, dwell on what could go wrong, and emotionally rehearse disappointment. Without realizing it, they are spending their most precious currency on poverty, failure, and regret. Because the Universe responds faithfully to the images impressed upon it, they receive in kind.

But you are not most people. You know the power of directing your imagination on purpose. You know that imagination is the soil where seeds of faith are planted, watered, and grown into towering oaks of reality. You know that to picture your dream as already real is to make a deposit that pays exponential interest.

Think about it this way: money is useful but limited. Imagination is infinite. With it, you can walk the halls of your dream home before the foundation is poured. You can run your fingers along the smooth railing of a staircase that hasn't yet been built. You can host the dinner party, hear the laughter, clink the glasses—all before the first guest has even been invited. Each of those images is a transaction in the unseen realm, securing the reality in advance.

I remember facing this question myself when I was imagining a second waterfront home. At first, I wasn't sure which image to focus on. Was it the deal being accepted? Was it signing the paperwork at the lawyer's office? None of those truly stirred the sense of ownership in me. They felt transactional, not transformational.

What finally clicked was much simpler and far more powerful. I pictured myself arriving home, putting my key into the door, opening it, and stepping inside. I let myself feel the weight of the key in my hand. I breathed in the scent of pine and the faint smoky trace from our last fire in the stone fireplace. I saw myself walking across the great room, hearing the creak of the floors under my feet. That was the image that brought the scene alive in me. That was the picture that made ownership feel natural, inevitable, and complete.

This is the fine distinction. The right image is the one that creates the strongest emotional connection to the end result. It may be the sound of loons on the lake, the smell of a campfire, the laughter of grandchildren splashing in the water, or the sight of a Christmas tree glowing in the window. For each person, the "currency" that feels most real will be different. The point is to play with your imagination until you discover the image that anchors you most deeply in the knowing that it is already yours.

Your imagination is also a training ground for faith. Every time you revisit the picture, every time you live it in detail, you are rehearsing your belief until it becomes automatic. Doubt cannot survive in a mind that is saturated with vivid, repeated images of the fulfilled desire. The more you dwell in imagination, the more natural your dream feels. The more natural it feels, the faster it arrives. As Neville Goddard wrote in *The Power of Awareness*, "How can this feeling of naturalness be achieved? The secret lies in one word: imagination."

Here is where the currency becomes magic: what you imagine with deep feeling impresses not only your own subconscious, but the very field of life itself. The Universe begins rearranging people, places, opportunities, and resources to match the blueprint you have drawn within. Invisible doors swing open. Seemingly random encounters appear. Surprising solutions arise. From the outside, it looks like coincidence. But from the inside, you know it is simply the return on your investment.

Treat imagination with reverence. Don't squander it on fear. Don't let it idle on trivial worries. Spend it boldly. Spend it deliberately. Paint pictures so real that you could reach out and touch them. Immerse yourself in the sensory richness of your desires fulfilled. See it, hear it, taste it, feel it. The more alive it is within, the sooner it takes shape without.

Think of this book as your permission slip to reenter the classroom of the soul. Here daydreaming is not punished; it is praised. Staring out the window of your mind is not idleness; it is training. Every image you allow yourself to hold, every scenario you dare to rehearse, is an act of creation. You are rebuilding the very muscle the world once told you to silence. Only this time, you are the teacher, and the subject is your own abundance.

Your imagination is not make-believe. It is creation in its earliest stage. Every time you engage it with intention, you are moving wealth from the invisible into the visible. That is the true currency of imagination: its ability to convert the unseen into the seen, the hoped-for into the lived.

Spend this currency lavishly. Spend it joyfully. Let your imagination run wild with abundance, with beauty, with love. When you do, you are not pretending—you are banking. And the return on this currency is limitless.

21

Play in Possibility

IN THE CHAPTER "REDUCE It to the Ridiculous," we explored how stretching your imagination to outrageous levels—$10 million, even $100 million—suddenly makes $1 million look small. That exercise isn't about crunching numbers. It's about shifting perspective. From a higher vantage point, everything looks different. When you elevate your thinking beyond what seems "reasonable," new possibilities begin to appear.

Most people confine their dreams to what they can rationally calculate or justify. They think in terms of what they've seen before, what others around them have achieved, or what seems "realistic." But every breakthrough that has ever reshaped the world was born from someone daring to step outside of logic and into the realm of pure possibility.

This is why I love the word *play*. Possibility is not supposed to feel heavy. It's not a burden or a checklist to conquer. It's a canvas of imagination, a field where you can run free without rules, limits, or predetermined outcomes. When you *play* in possibility, you give your mind permission to create without consequence. It doesn't need to add up right now. It doesn't need to be practical. It simply needs to be alive.

I remember working privately with a client who came to me with a goal of generating $1 million in her business. When I asked her what that would actually look like—after expenses, after travel (first-class flights, five-star hotels, the lifestyle she truly wanted)—she admitted she hadn't really thought about it in detail. She was more focused on what she believed she could generate, not on what she actually wanted to generate.

That's the trap many people fall into: they aim for what feels "possible" based on their current perspective rather than playing in true possibility. So I suggested she think bigger. Much bigger. Instead of setting a $1 million revenue goal, I encouraged her to set a profitable revenue goal of $10 million, with her personal income exceeding $1s million if that's what she wanted. Of course, she did want that. She just hadn't dared to claim it.

The shift in her energy was immediate. Suddenly she wasn't thinking in terms of limits; she was thinking in terms of desire. She began to imagine what her business could look like if she allowed herself to scale to that level. She lit up with ideas, opportunities, and strategies that had never occurred to her before. She stopped confining herself to "reasonable" and started playing in "possible."

When you think of $1 million, your mind might still whisper words like "hard," "rare," or "difficult." But when you play at $100 million, you're forced into a space where you cannot possibly figure out all the steps. That's where possibility takes over. That's where the mind surrenders its limitations and imagination kicks in.

This chapter is your invitation to do the same. Play bigger. Dream beyond what feels safe or comfortable. Write down ideas that feel ridiculous. Ask yourself: *If nothing was impossible, what would I* *create? If I already had unlimited resources, how would I live? If I were to design a plan for $100 million, what would it look like?*

The beauty of this practice is not in the number itself but in the expansion it generates. Because the moment you stretch into bigger ideas, the smaller goals no longer feel intimidating. A million looks small when you've trained your imagination on $100 million. Just as a runner who trains with weights on their ankles finds it effortless to run free, your mind becomes stronger when it's exercised in vast possibility.

You don't need to know *how* it will all come about. This isn't about building a business plan for investors or convincing anyone of your worthiness. This is about playing—expanding the borders of your belief system so wide that the very idea of "impossible" loses its meaning.

Your desires don't need to fit neatly inside the lines of what your logic can handle today. They only need you to give them air, attention, and freedom. Play in possibility, and you'll discover that the Universe itself loves to play back.

As I shared in my book *The Moment of Alignment*, "What you accept as possible sets the boundaries of your reality. Expand your belief, and your world expands with it."

22

Anchor the Identity

EVERY DESIRE YOU HOLD—THE millions in your account, the home on the water, the freedom to give generously, the success that seems almost too grand to imagine—is asking you for one thing: to become the person who already has it.

This is the part of manifestation that many people overlook. They think it's about waiting for evidence, for signs, for circumstances to shift. They believe that if they work hard enough, the Universe will eventually reward them with proof.

The truth is the opposite: the external world cannot shift until you do. The magnet is who you are being in every moment. The most extraordinary truth of all is that when you anchor your identity in the version of yourself who already lives your desire, life cannot help but reorganize itself around that vibration.

There are really two versions of you. One version still sees your dream as something "out there," something you are working toward, something that might or might not arrive. This version of you watches your bank account for reassurance, measures your worth by numbers, and scrolls real estate listings with the whisper of "someday." You want it, but you do not yet feel it as yours.

The other version of you already belongs in the life you envision. You don't wait for money to appear before you feel wealthy; you treat yourself and your decisions as though wealth is natural. You don't need the deed in hand before you feel at home; you walk through your day as if you are already the individual who lives there.

Both versions are you, yet they live in entirely different realities. The outcomes follow the identity that is most consistently embodied.

When I guide my clients into anchoring their new identity, I often give them a simple four-step framework.

1. Decide what you would truly love. Clarity is power, but vagueness keeps you circling in indecision.
2. Determine what you would need to believe in order for that desire to be yours. This is where self-concept comes into play. Do you believe you are capable? Do you believe you are worthy? Do you believe you are enough—smart enough, young enough, experienced enough?
3. Engage your senses. What would you see, hear, smell, taste, and touch if your desire were already fulfilled? The more vividly you live it in your imagination, the more naturally it begins to feel real.
4. Live as if it is already done. Each morning, before your feet touch the floor, choose to be the version of yourself who already has what you desire. Walk through your day as that individual. That choice, repeated with consistency, cements the identity until it becomes second nature.

This is why the greatest treasure in any goal is not the result itself but who you become in the process of claiming it. Bold desires stretch you. They call forth strength, courage, imagination, and faith that may have been dormant until now. They ask you to shed the limitations of the old self and grow into the higher self who can hold and sustain them.

That stretch is not a punishment; it is the gift. Because once you become that individual, no result can be taken from you. The millions may come and go. The house may be bought and sold. But who you are becoming in the process—someone who trusts imagination more than fear, who holds faith more firmly than doubt, who makes decisions as if their desires are already fulfilled—that is yours forever.

Anchoring identity is not about pretending or playing make-believe. It is about living in advance of the evidence. You begin to walk, talk, and choose as the version of yourself who already holds what you desire. You notice the language you use and shift it from "if" to "when," from "someday" to "now." You carry yourself with the quiet authority of someone who no longer doubts their worth. You make decisions, even small ones, from abundance rather than scarcity. With each consistent choice, the identity takes root until it feels more natural to live as your fulfilled self than as your old self.

The old identity will resist. It will clamor for proof. It will say, "Show me the money, then I'll feel wealthy. Show me the acceptance letter, then I'll feel chosen. Show me the opportunity, then I'll believe I'm worthy." But faith works the other way. Faith says, "Feel it now, and the proof will come."

You don't conquer fear by wrestling with it. You anchor a new identity by practicing faith until it feels more natural than doubt. When it feels natural—when it feels like memory—it becomes the foundation on which your world is built.

That is why anchoring the identity is not a small step or a side practice. It is the entire path. It is the work of becoming who you truly are. The more you claim that identity, the more everything in your outer world falls into place to match.

23

Wealth Anchors

AWARENESS IS THE BIRTHPLACE of transformation. It is the quiet yet undeniable recognition of who you are and the infinite power you carry within. This is easy to forget in the hustle of daily life. Fear surges. Doubt creeps in. Old stories whisper, "You can't." Before you know it, you're swept into the current of struggle.

This forgetting is not failure. It is simply part of being human. Life often feels like a roller coaster: dips and turns are inevitable on the climb toward greater expansion. The key is not to avoid them; the key is to shorten the distance between forgetting and remembering. Develop the reflex of returning to awareness quickly, repeatedly, until alignment becomes your natural home.

I often tell my clients: "Fear only has power when you forget who you are." The moment you remember, fear dissolves. Alignment is never far away: it is always only one breath, one thought, one choice away.

One of the most effective ways to return to awareness is by creating what I call *alignment anchors*. Anchors are simple cues that pull you back into alignment in the middle of ordinary life. They transform everyday moments into sacred reminders of who you truly are.

You don't need to wait for meditation, journaling, or quiet reflection to realign. You can weave alignment into the fabric of your day by linking it to things you're already doing. These anchors become triggers for remembrance. For example:

Every time your phone chimes with a notification, instead of letting it pull you into distraction, let it snap you back into alignment. One sound—one breath—one return to *I am wealthy. I am aligned.*

Every time you pick up your pen, your glasses, or your keys, let it remind you: *I live in abundance now.*

Jewelry can become sacred anchors. A ring, a bracelet, a necklace—each time you touch it, you anchor back into the frequency of wealth, health, or peace.

Breath anchors are some of the most powerful. Every inhale and exhale can become a rhythm of remembrance: *with this breath, I feel abundant/wealthy/rich.* Since we breathe all day long, this anchor offers hundreds of opportunities to realign without effort.

Walking anchors transform the simple act of moving through your day. With every step, you can affirm: *I am wealthy* or *I am a millionaire.* Imagine the compound power of thousands of steps each day, each one carrying the vibration of alignment.

I created one of my earliest anchoring practices back in the 1990s. Every time I saw my reflection—in a mirror, a shop window, even the glass of a car door—I would say to myself: *"I see a happy and healthy multimillionaire."* It was simple. It was consistent. And it worked. That phrase imprinted itself so deeply that it became my truth. What began as an affirmation turned into an identity.

Matti, one of my Club Aligned members, recently shared a beautiful anchor she created: stoplights. Every time she's waiting at a red light, instead of growing impatient, she uses it as a cue to align. She breathes. She remembers. She affirms. In doing so, she transforms what most people see as wasted time into a moment of power.

Anchors don't have to be elaborate. In fact, the simpler, the better. The key is consistency. The more you repeat the practice, the more your subconscious links the trigger (the phone chime, the step, the pen in your hand) with the state of alignment. Over time, the anchor becomes automatic.

Think of awareness as a muscle. It strengthens with use. At first, returning to awareness may feel effortful. You may forget for hours, even days. But with anchors, you train yourself to return more quickly. The dips in the roller coaster become less steep, the climbs smoother.

Each time you choose awareness over fear, you build momentum. Each time you pause, breathe, and remember, you strengthen the baseline of faith. Over time, faith becomes your natural state. From that state, life flows. Ideas arrive. Money circulates. Opportunities appear.

You don't need to eliminate every doubt or silence every fear. You simply need to return, again and again, until alignment outweighs misalignment, until remembering becomes more natural than forgetting.

Here's the beauty: your anchors are yours to design. Choose one. Choose many. Tie them to the rhythms of your day. Each anchor is a doorway back to who you really are.

Imagine living this way: each time your phone chimes, you return. Each time you breathe, you return. Each time you step forward, you return. Soon life itself becomes your meditation. Awareness is no longer something you visit: it is where you live.

From that steady state of awareness, prosperity is not something you chase. It is something you host. Wealth becomes natural. Miracles become ordinary. And making a million look small becomes not just a concept but your lived reality.

24

Act As If, Live As Now

THERE COMES A POINT in every manifestation journey where the imagination is no longer something you simply visit in quiet moments of meditation or visualization: it becomes the air you breathe.

The practice of "acting as if" is not about pretending or playacting in a shallow way. It is about entering into the felt reality of your desire now, in the most tangible and embodied way possible, so that every part of you begins to resonate with it as truth.

When you act *as if*, you stop waiting for evidence to give you permission to feel wealthy, loved, free, or abundant. You decide that the state of being belongs to you now. Then, with that decision made, you live it.

This is not recklessness; it is alignment. Recklessness ignores reality and leaps without grounding. Alignment allows you to step into the vibration of your desire safely, wisely, and joyfully, and it costs you nothing but a willingness to play.

Go to the open houses of homes that mirror the kind of beauty and expansiveness you desire. Walk through those rooms as though you already hold the keys. Run your hands along the banisters, pause at the windows, and look out as if the view belongs to you. Don't just observe: own the experience.

Go to the car dealership and sit in the driver's seat of the luxury car that stirs something inside of you. Close your eyes, feel the leather beneath your fingertips, breathe in the scent of newness, and imagine the hum of the engine as yours. Let your body register the reality before your mind tries to reason it away.

Go into the designer boutique you once only passed by. Step inside. Touch the fabrics, feel the textures, try on an outfit that calls to you. Look in the mirror and see not someone hoping to afford it someday but the person who has already expanded into that level of lifestyle. It costs you nothing to try it on, but it reconditions your subconscious to believe that this reality is natural for you.

These acts are not about convincing yourself with effort. They are about collapsing the distance between the desire and the embodiment. The subconscious does not distinguish between "real" and "imagined" when the feelings are sincere.

By immersing yourself in experiences that mirror your vision, you build the naturalness Neville Goddard spoke of—that sweet familiarity where your dream feels less like fantasy and more like memory.

Some will tell you to wait until you can afford it, until the money shows up, until you've proven yourself ready. But if you wait for proof, you'll wait forever. Proof comes after belief, not before.

When you live as now, you declare that the blessing is already yours. You treat yourself as the one who has already arrived. You walk differently. You talk differently. You choose differently. Even if your outer circumstances are still catching up, your inner world has already shifted, and the outer must always follow.

This includes how you relate to money itself. If you were already living as a multimillionaire, how would you interact with it? Would you ignore it until it piled up, or would you begin engaging with it intentionally, wisely, and confidently? A multimillionaire doesn't just spend: they also steward, allocate, and invest. Acting *as if* means stepping into that level of relationship with money now.

You don't have to wait until millions are sitting in your account to begin. You can start today by preparing your mind, your habits, and your decisions for the wealth you are calling in.

Ask yourself:

What if I treated my current savings account as though it were a million-dollar portfolio? Would I ignore it, or would I review it carefully, strategizing how to grow it?

What if I began studying investment opportunities—real estate, stocks, businesses, or philanthropy—so that when the money arrives, I already know how to use it?

What if I designed a giving plan today, imagining the scholarships, charities, or causes I'll joyfully fund?

What if I explored recurring revenue models, licensing, or membership sites and practiced seeing myself as the person experiencing ongoing abundance?

These aren't idle exercises. They are rehearsals for inevitability. Each step you take like this conditions your subconscious to accept the role of someone who not only receives wealth but multiplies it. You dissolve the old patterns of "I wouldn't know what to do if I had it" and replace them with "I already know how to live at that level."

When readiness meets opportunity, results appear with speed and precision. Money responds to the vibration of responsibility and expansion. You are no longer waiting to become ready. You are training readiness into your identity now.

This is the art of acting *as if*: dissolving the gap between imagination and reality by embodying the knowing that it is done, here, now.

Ask yourself: where could you begin to step into your desire today? Where could you bring your body, your senses, your emotions into contact with the reality you've already claimed within? Play with it. Enjoy it. Expand into it. The more you live it now, the faster it materializes into form.

Every act of alignment is a rehearsal for inevitability. Each step you take as if it's already yours builds a rhythm, a resonance, a naturalness that leaves no room for doubt. This isn't play-pretend. It's power. It's the shaping of reality through the steady embodiment of what already exists in the unseen.

As the inspirational author Dorothea Brande so wisely said, "Act as if it were impossible to fail." When you live this way—when you walk into every room, every store, every vision with that kind of certainty—you will discover that what once felt extraordinary becomes your ordinary.

25

Celebrate before Arrival

THERE IS A SECRET the world rarely teaches: celebration is not something you save for the finish line. It is a power you invoke at the starting line. Celebration is not an afterthought. It is fuel, magnetism, and declaration all in one. When you celebrate in advance, you shift from longing to living. You step into the energy of your dream as though it were already complete.

I've done this countless times. When I planned the party and sent out invitations for my new waterfront home before the closing papers were signed, I wasn't pretending; I was practicing alignment. I was saying to myself and to the Universe, "This is done. I am ready." With the act of preparing and decorating in my imagination and picturing guests walking through the front door, my belief deepened into certainty.

I remember buying the dress I would wear to an awards banquet long before the award was officially mine. That gown hung in my closet like a promise, not of what might be, but of what already was in the unseen. I also created the sign for my office door that read "Dr. Peggy McColl" before I had ever held my diploma. Each time I looked at that sign, I felt the pride, the gratitude, the completion.

I even planned the graduation celebration before the degree was in hand. To an outside observer, these things may have looked bold, even irrational. But to me, they were natural extensions of knowing.

I've watched my clients do the same. One woman bought her wedding dress before she had even met her husband, not as an act of desperation, but as a radiant expression of faith. She aligned with the joy of that day so completely that the external form had no choice but to catch up. And of course it did. She is now happily married to the man she envisioned herself walking toward.

Celebration in advance is not about living recklessly. It's not about spending money you don't have or forcing a result into existence. It's about inhabiting the energy of the fulfilled desire so vividly that the world must rearrange itself to meet you there. When you celebrate, you are broadcasting certainty. You are saying, "This is mine, I am grateful, and I am already enjoying it."

This is how you collapse time. Gratitude in advance is one of the most powerful catalysts of manifestation. Celebration draws the future into the present and makes it feel natural. By celebrating now, you transform waiting into receiving. You walk around in the atmosphere of fulfillment, and from that place, inspired action flows effortlessly.

Ask yourself: *how can I celebrate before arrival?* Perhaps it's planning the party, choosing the outfit, ordering the champagne glasses, designing the logo, or framing the cover of the book you know you will publish. Maybe it's practicing your victory speech in the mirror or creating a space in your home for the award you know is already yours. The form doesn't matter; the energy does.

When you celebrate in advance, you dissolve doubt. You embody joy. You stand in the truth of your desire with such clarity that the world must answer.

26

The Million Made Small

THERE WAS A TIME when a million dollars felt like a mountain. It was untouchable, almost mythical—an idea that lived far outside the edges of possibility. Maybe it even intimidated you, standing there on the horizon like a summit only "special" people could reach. But here's the truth: a million is not a mountain. It is a pebble. It is a single stepping stone in the river of creation that flows endlessly toward you, through you, *as* you.

The power of alignment has made what once looked enormous now feel inevitable. That is the great paradox of manifestation: what begins as an audacious dream—something outrageous, unattainable, almost laughable—becomes natural, normal, and even small once it is embodied. The same number that used to feel colossal shrinks in the light of your new identity. Because the million is not the prize. The million is not the goal. The million is simply a mirror reflecting back who you dared to become.

And who have you become? Someone who no longer negotiates with doubt. Someone who doesn't tiptoe around desire but claims it boldly, completely. Someone who understands that imagination is not a toy but the most sacred currency of creation. Someone who has learned to relax in the knowing, to celebrate before the arrival, to live "as if" until the line between vision and fact has blurred into one seamless reality.

This is what happens when you make faith your home. The external evidence may have lagged at first, but it could not resist the weight of your alignment. Reality had no choice but to bend toward the truth you declared within. You didn't chase the million: you became the person who naturally generates, attracts, and multiplies it. Now the million has become a small thing.

Here's the gift hidden inside this realization: if $1 million can be made small, then so can $10 million, or $100 million, or any other vision that whispers in the chambers of your heart. There is no ceiling except the one you build with disbelief. There are no limits but the ones you accept. The game of expansion never ends, because you are infinite consciousness clothed in human form.

And yet—pause here—this is not about numbers at all. The million is symbolic. It is shorthand for your wildest dreams, your most expansive self-expression. The same principles that carried you here will carry you into the next horizon and the one after that. Once you've proven to yourself that what was once "too big" is actually small, you are free. You are unshackled from the illusion of limitation. You walk the earth as someone who knows: *everything is already mine*.

Making a million look small isn't the end of the story—it's the beginning. This is not theory, not wishful thinking, not a collection of pretty concepts. It is a living practice. Alignment is not something you dabble in; it is who you are. It is a way of being that calls you to show up, every single day, as the person who already has what you desire.

Abundance is not an event. It is not a windfall or a lucky break. It is a rhythm—a way of moving through life with gratitude as your foundation, faith as your atmosphere, and imagination as your constant companion. You notice evidence of abundance everywhere—in the smallest coin, the unexpected kindness, the opportunity that seems to appear out of nowhere. You celebrate it all, because what you honor multiplies.

When you live this way, miracles no longer shock you. They become your normal. You don't wait for permission. You grant it. You don't shrink when fear shows up. You feed your faith instead. You expand, you circulate, you grow yourself bigger than the numbers until numbers no longer intimidate you: they follow you.

To anchor this knowing into your very cells, I leave you with words to declare aloud every single day—not as a wish, but as truth. Speak them as your identity, as who you already are:

MY DAILY WAY OF BEING

I am wealthy.

I am abundant.

I am aligned.

I am the living embodiment of prosperity. Every thought I think, every word I speak, and every action I take flows from the certainty that it is already done.

I am relaxed in knowing that all I desire is mine now. I rest in the naturalness of my dreams fulfilled, and I carry myself with the ease and confidence of the one who has already received it.

I am richly provided for, in ways seen and unseen.

Opportunities, resources, and connections flow to me easily. I am always in the right place, at the right time, meeting the right people.

I am a magnet for miracles, and I expect them. I celebrate in advance, I give thanks in the now, and I delight in the continuous unfolding of greater and greater good.

I am faith in motion. I choose to see with the eyes of possibility, to feed the flame of imagination, and to dwell in the vibration of completion.

I am the person who lives the life I once dreamed of—and more. I am the evidence that alignment works, that imagination is currency, and that wealth is simply my natural way of being.

I am wealth.

I am abundance.

I am alignment.

I am.

Note from the Author

As you turn the final page of this book, I want to pause and say thank you. Thank you for trusting me to walk beside you through these ideas, these practices, and these truths. It has been my honor to share what I know to be the most powerful wisdom in the world: that you are the creator of your own reality, and that abundance is already yours.

I don't take this lightly. I feel an overwhelming sense of gratitude to serve you in this way. My hope is that these words don't just live on the page, but that they live in you—that they guide your choices, shape your faith, and expand what you allow yourself to believe is possible.

I would love to hear your story. How has this book affected you? What results have you seen? How has your life changed as you've stepped into alignment and made a million look small? Please share with me: I would be delighted to celebrate with you. You can reach me and my team at support@peggymccoll.com.

As you move forward, remember that you already hold within you everything required to live the life you love. You are powerful beyond measure, and the Universe is conspiring in your favor.

With love, deep gratitude and unwavering belief in you,

Peggy

About the Author

DR. PEGGY McCOLL IS a world-renowned wealth, manifestation, and success mentor who has dedicated more than four decades to helping individuals across the globe make their dreams a reality. She has inspired millions to expand their vision, unlock prosperity, and live fully aligned lives of abundance, joy, and fulfillment.

A *New York Times* bestselling author, Peggy has written twenty-six transformational books—translated into multiple languages and read in nearly 100 countries—touching the hearts and minds of readers everywhere.

As the founder of a thriving international business, Peggy has guided clients to shift their beliefs, align with their desires, and manifest results beyond what they once thought possible. Her unique teachings blend timeless metaphysical principles with practical strategies, earning her recognition as one of the most sought-after mentors in the field of personal growth and wealth consciousness.

Peggy's unwavering belief in the power of imagination, faith, and alignment is the cornerstone of her own success and the success of those she mentors. Through her programs, masterminds, and private mentoring, she continues to show others how to make even a million look small—by first expanding who they believe themselves to be.

When she isn't writing or mentoring, Peggy embraces a joy-filled life with her husband, Denis, cherishes time with her son, Michel, daughter-in-law, Kayla, and precious grandchildren, James and Aria, and enjoys the beauty of the simple beauty of home, nature and family.

For free gifts and resources, visit www.PeggyMcColl.com.

www.ingramcontent.com/pod-product-compliance
Lightning Source LLC
Chambersburg PA
CBHW072157070526
44585CB00015B/1177